Introduction to Living Well

Dennis E. Bradford, Ph.D.

Legalities

ISBN 978-1940487205

Conesus Lake, New York   24 September 2019

Contents

Preface

Although living well is simple, it's not easy. Just understanding that statement requires some good thinking with respect to the chief obstacle that prevents living well, namely, attachment to, or identification with, thinking. The best procedure is, first, understand the necessity for disidentifying with thinking for anyone who wants to live well and, second, break that attachment.

Serious thinking is hard work. However, being lazy and avoiding it doesn't work well. All that happens to people who do that is that they get stuck in whatever conceptual system or ideology they were brought up in, which means that they settle for enduring all the same problems their parents and other ancestors did.

Furthermore, it's not necessary to be an intellectual, either. In fact, as I argue in what follows, just like any other attachment, attachment to incessant thinking obstructs living well.

There is a middle way. Think hard when it's necessary or valuable and, otherwise, don't.

If you have not yet thought hard about how to live well or wisely and not yet uncovered for yourself a way to create a meaningful life, now's the time to think hard – briefly!

This is not a long work. However, in it, it's my intention to offer you the best results of all the hard thinking I've done about how to live better since I committed myself to being a philosopher in 1964. I hope that you find that, even if you judge some of the ideas here to be wrong after understanding them, you'll at least find some of them to be useful and very beneficial.

It's not my intention that you attach to my thoughts. Instead, test them for yourself. If they make sense, adopt them. If they don't, find better ones. The purpose of this work is simply to shorten your learning curve, to make it easier for you to adopt practices that will enable you to live better.

This work is a companion to my *Stress Reduction Wizardry* video trainings. It presupposes that you have understood some of the important distinctions made there such as the distinction between demonstrative and nondemonstrative evidence. It's critical that you have actually begun some daily practice such as Aliveness Awareness that's effective. Doing that is much more important than reading or even studying this essay.

As in that training, you may learn the ideas offered here more efficiently if you do not begin at the beginning and proceed to go through them in order to the end. That's especially true if you are not a *What? learner*. The first two sections, namely, *The Big Picture* and *Introduction to Living Well Spiritually* are the most difficult to understand. They are the most abstract and mention important ideas with which you may not already be familiar. For that reason, you might want to begin with whichever of the other sections that interests you most and come back to the first two sections later. However, since the first two sections are the most important sections, please don't ignore them.

Even if you don't yet believe it, assume that *you are infinitely valuable*. Realizing for yourself that infinite value is the real topic of this work. Enjoy!

Acute Suffering

If you are depressed or suicidal, you are not in a position to enjoy this or any other work. If you want to live well, you have two tasks.

First, get back to normal. Acute dissatisfaction is different from normal dissatisfaction. If you are acutely dissatisfied for any reason, please get some help. If you are unable to find a suitable psychiatrist, clinical psychologist, or consulting philosopher, find a spiritual counselor or even a good friend. Life is difficult. If it has knocked you down, that doesn't mean that there's something inherently wrong with you. In fact, there is nothing inherently wrong with you [as I explain in what follows]. For now, just get some help to get back up on your feet.

Second, begin the transition from normal dissatisfaction to living well. When you are back on your feet, use this and similar books and resources to continue your progress towards mastering life.

Since we are in the middle of them, it's difficult to obtain perspective on our own lives. As a bonus, as long as I'm available, you may have a no-cost, no-obligation, one-on-one, 15-minute phone or Skype call with me. If you are interested and live in North America, go to: https://calendly.com/dennis-47/15 and schedule a call. We could discuss your single most important problem and, although you should not expect a solution in a brief phone call, perhaps I may be able to direct you towards a solution.

With respect to **depression**, are you depressed? Have you recently been in a depressed mood most of the time nearly every day? Have you recently had diminished interest or enjoyment in normal activities most of the time nearly every day? Has your body weight recently dropped due to poor appetite or has it gone up due to increased appetite? Are you having difficulty sleeping or sleeping too much? Have you lost energy? Are you fatigued? Do you feel worthless, excessively guilty, or hopeless? Has your ability to concentrate diminished? Do you recurrently think about death or suicide?

If your answers to some of these questions are affirmative, you may be suffering from major depression (or even undiagnosed major depression), which is a common disorder in our society. That's typically a temporary condition that's not your fault. Since, fortunately, it's usually an eminently treatable disorder that often has serious consequences, please be kind to yourself and seek clinical treatment. (Incidentally, in the long term, nothing—I believe—will be more valuable for you than the kind of "spiritual" prescription I recommend in what follows.)

Also, the booklist at the end of Mastery in 7 Steps has some very helpful readings about curing mood disorders. It may surprise you to learn that some have physical causes that can be treated by something as simple as targeted, temporary supplementation and a permanently improved diet. [Also see "Introduction to Living Well Physically" below.]

With respect to **suicide**, are you suicidal? You're at increased risk if you have suffered family trauma, unstabilized turmoil, domestic violence, physical or sexual abuse, loss of a family member, feelings of being a burden, or had an alcoholic parent. Are you depressed? Do you feel hopeless?

Associated contributing factors may be indicated by affirmative answers to *any* of the following questions: Are you isolated or withdrawn? Do you use alcohol, marijuana, cocaine, opioids, or other psychoactive drugs that have not been prescribed for you? If you are a student, is your academic performance poor? Do you frequently get into disputes with your peers? Have you been disappointed romantically? Are you worried about pregnancy, sexual orientation, or AIDS?

Are you upset about the suicide of any friends, peers, or family members? Do you suffer from cancer, Huntington's disease, multiple sclerosis, or anorexia nervosa? Have you had a head or spinal cord injury? Have you ever attempted suicide?

Suicidal crises are episodic. Definitive treatment does cause them to pass. If you find yourself thinking about suicide, please be kind to yourself and seek expert help. Treat such obstacles as opportunities to teach yourself how to live better. You are capable of living well, so why not teach yourself how? If you do, you'll not only benefit yourself, but also you'll be able to show others how to help themselves.

You may not yet realize it, but, as I explain in what follows, **you are infinitely valuable and we need you.** Since that is so, suicidal thoughts are ultimately delusional.

❖

The Big Picture

The idea that living well is fulfilling our potential goes back in western philosophy at least as far as Aristotle. If we don't fulfill our potential, how could we justifiably feel that we have lived well or are living well? Let's assume that to live well is to fulfill our potential.

However, what does that mean? Without specifying what it means, it's too general, too abstract, to be useful. Let's, then, ask the question, '**What is a fulfilled human being?**'

It's impossible coherently to answer that question without answering two logically prior questions, namely, 'What is a human being?' and 'What is fulfillment?'

It's not really helpful to claim that **fulfilment** is realizing our potential. Why? As Jean-Paul Sartre has pointed out, there's no way to determine potential. How can we single it out for our attention? Which object is it? The idea of potential goes with vague, general ideas like excellence or quality. What is an excellent human being?

In certain domains it's possible to determine criteria of excellence. For example, achieving at least a 1200-pound total (classically, a 500-pound deadlift, a 400-pound squat, and a 300-pound bench press) is sufficient for being considered strong, for enjoying excellent strength and the ability to demonstrate it. What, though, might it mean to fulfill our nature outside of all such specific domains? No coherent answer can be given without answering the question about the nature of being human.

What is a **human being**? Since we are human beings, this is an obviously important question to answer. It's impossible to understand what a fulfilled human being is without understanding what a human being is.

There are a lot of different theories about what it means to be a human being. These theories themselves ground different theories about ethics, political philosophy, psychology, and many other disciplines. Intellectuals tend to attach themselves to one theory or other about human nature and then work out an understanding of its consequences in other areas.

In my experience, most people are simply confused about their own nature. It's not so much that they are wrong in what they believe about themselves; instead, it's that their beliefs about themselves are radically incomplete.

Suppose I were to ask you, 'Who are you?' If you answered, you'd likely answer by giving me your autobiography, the story of your life from its beginning until now. You might tell me about your parents, your upbringing, your formal education, your relationships, your fears and hopes about the future, and so on. If you answered in that way, your (probably implicit) answer would be that you are the person who had all those experiences.

Suppose, though, that I were to ask you, 'What is a person?' In other words, 'What kind of thing is an individual human being?' I might ask, 'Who, really, are you?' meaning 'Which individual human being are you? In what does your uniqueness consist?'

There are two logically fundamental questions here. First, how do we, or how should we, understand kinds of objects? Second, how do we, or how should we, understand individuals?

At this point, if it hasn't already, the patience of nonphilosophers usually runs out. The word 'philosopher' means 'lover of wisdom.' If we equate living wisely with living well, **a philosopher is simply someone who is serious about living well**.

We are not born understanding how to live well. It's also not obvious how to live well; there are many conflicting ideas about it.

Here's where the problem of expertise comes in. Suppose that your house has a plumbing problem and you are not a plumber. Not being an expert yourself, how do you determine who is a good plumber to contact to fix that problem? When we lack an expert's understanding in some domain, how do we tell who is a genuine expert in that domain? It's impossible to become an expert in every domain. Generally, we rely on the testimony of others to provide a practical solution that can work to solve some relevant problem.

When it comes to the topic of living well, who should we contact? Who is an expert on living well? There's a lot of disagreement. Furthermore, it's not only that we don't know who to contact, but it's a really important problem.

The best solution is to *think through the alternatives for yourself.* That's difficult, but at least if you do so you'll be in charge of your own life, your own values, and not have to rely on dubitable suggestions from others. If you have the courage to think hard coupled with the curiosity of an open mind and the determination to learn from mistakes about how to live better, you are ripe for philosophy.

Are you a philosopher? I hope so. Otherwise, unless it can happen by luck or magic, you'll never live well. If that sounds harsh, please think of it as tough love.

Philosophy begins with wonder, specifically, with wondering about how to live better. In Part Four of <u>Sapiens</u>, Y. N. Harari emphasizes how critical the discovery of ignorance has been for our civilization. Similarly, it's critical for anyone wanting to live well to detach from whatever unexamined beliefs that were uncritically absorbed in childhood.

If life is worth living, it's worth living well. Notice that it's not necessary to have studied philosophy formally to be a philosopher. All that's necessary is to be committed to living well and to investigating it for yourself. Philosophers live examined lives. If you are seriously committed to improving the quality of your life, you won't become impatient when investigating important or fundamental questions.

Back to the previous dialectic. How do we understand **kinds** of objects? In western philosophy, it was Aristotle who first clarified the answer. It's by noting relevant similarities and differences.

For example, suppose that you are hungry and lost in the woods. You come upon something that might be edible. What, you ask yourself, kind of thing is this? You examine it and decide that it must be a fruit of some kind. If you are able to determine its similarities and differences to other kinds of fruit that you already understand, you may be able to determine whether or not it is poisonous, whether or not it is ripe, and so on. Once you make those determinations and understand better what it is, you'll be in a better position to make a rational decision about whether or not to eat it. You don't need to become a scientific expert on fruits to decide whether or not to eat it, but, since some fruits may make you ill, assuming you had much choice you'd be foolish to eat it without some understanding of its nature or qualities.

If so, we come to understand kinds by noting their similarities and differences to other previously understood kinds. We use analogies to increase our conceptual understanding.

(You might next wonder: 'How do we begin to understand? How is it possible to improve our understanding before we have analogies to use?' If you thought of those questions on your own, that demonstrates a talent for fundamental thinking. The answer is as fascinating as it is important, but, since I've discussed it elsewhere in writing and it would lead us too far astray, let's proceed here without discussing it.)

Next question: How do we understand individuals?

It's critical in this context to distinguish an **individual** from its qualities. A quality is a commonality, a feature or property that two or more individuals may share or have in common. For example, redness is a quality; two or more individuals may be red.

Back to your individuality: What makes you you? What is distinctive about you? What identifies or individuates you? What makes you unique?

Could it be, for example, the color of your hair? Well, no, it can't be any such quality. Why? Two or more individual humans may share the same hair color.

Could it be, for example, the combination of all your qualities? That's an interesting question.

There's a difference between "monadic" qualities, which may be had by one individual, and "relational" qualities, which can only be had by two or more individuals. Color is a monadic quality. For example, a shirt may be red. Leftness is a relational quality. It's impossible for a shirt to be to the left of itself, although, of course, with two shirts one can be to the left of the other.

Could your set of monadic qualities make you you? Could that explain your uniqueness? In practice, your set of monadic qualities may be unique. In fact, you may be the only human being in the world with your specific set of monadic qualities.

However, that answer is theoretically unsatisfactory. Why? There could be two individuals who share all the same monadic qualities. Two balls, for example, could have exactly the same color, size, chemical composition, texture, and so on. There's no logical reason why two different human beings couldn't share exactly the same set of monadic qualities.

Perhaps, then, your unique set of relational qualities is what makes you you? After all, you and only you have, for example, your spatial, temporal, and other relational qualities. They are unique to you. However, philosophers ask, 'Is your unique set of relational qualities what makes you you or is your having a unique set of relational qualities the result of your preexisting uniqueness?'

Furthermore, your unique position in space and time seems accidental. Is that all that makes you you? In other words, is your essence, your whatness, nothing but an accident?

Furthermore, your ultimate reality as an individual would then depend upon the reality of space and time. Some serious philosophers such as mystics and contemporary physicists who accept quantum entanglement deny that space and time are ultimately real (which is why that spooky immediate action at a distance that Einstein so disliked may actually be a feature of physical reality). If so, depending upon spatial and temporal relations to individuate you would undermine your ultimate reality.

Of course, many people, including Einstein, have been terminally attached conceptually and psychologically to the ultimate reality of space and time. However, attachment to a proposition is never a justification for it. In fact, it seems that quantum entanglement is real although, like all scientific claims, the evidence for that statement is nondemonstrative. This is a topic in both the philosophy of science and the philosophy of mathematics. It's one of understanding the conceptual cash value of the equations of, say, string theory, which is a candidate for a universal field theory. Furthermore, although dark energy and dark matter are currently thought to make up 96% of the universe, physicists currently lack a clear understanding of either. The stars make up only about 4% and higher elements like us make up only about .03%. Such facts can serve to keep us humble as we wonder about the world.

Whether you think this state of affairs interesting or a mess depends upon your perspective. Since serious thinking is difficult, most people seem to try to do as little of it as possible.

Concepts are principles of classification. If you are able to separate red objects from objects that aren't red, then you have the concept of redness.

Once you realize the nature of concepts, you realize why there must be a problem about understanding individuality (particularity, uniqueness). Since concepts are general, how could there be a concept of your individuality? [Incidentally, the topic of generality is an interesting topic in academic philosophy. As my favorite contemporary thinker and dissertation director Panayot Butchvarov has argued, another of my favorite philosophy professors, Gustav Bergmann, has had some very interesting ideas about the nature of generality.]

It's a distinct possibility, then, that any conceptual answer to the question, 'Who am I?' will be ultimately unsatisfactory. Perhaps this result may not be so surprising. The real issue is understanding your existence in reality, not your existence in thought. Obviously, there's an important difference between something's being real and it's only being thought to be real.

Now that we've noticed it as well as the difficulty of answering it conceptually, let's agree to leave open for now the question of your true nature. [I return to this point in what follows.] Notice that it might even be the case that, ultimately, and this may initially strike you as crazy, your existence as an individual person should be questioned. [The issue regarding the nature of personal identity is an issue in philosophy; there are, for example, anthologies of papers by philosophers with different and conflicting views. There's no quick, easy, or agreed-upon answer.]

This is not to suggest that you stop inquiring. By all means continue to ask, 'Who am I?' The takeaway here is just to be skeptical of any conceptual answer to it. Perhaps no conceptual answer could be satisfactory. Perhaps the answer is nonconceptual.

If reflections like these are on the right track, providing a conceptual answer to the question about your individuality may be difficult or impossible, but understanding your kind (nature, essence, whatness) is possible by noting relevant similarities and differences. There's universal agreement that you are a human being. As such, there should be paradigms or excellent examples of human beings, namely, those sages who live well or who are wise.

Is there a way to link the idea of living well with the idea of being human? Is there a way to identify those among us who are wise?

There is.

The key to making it a useful idea is simply to pay attention to the ordinary distinction between **being** and **doing**. Let's relate the correct description of you as a human being to that distinction. That will enable us to think clearly about excellent being and excellent doing.

Let's associate the phrase 'human being' with being and doing by relating, naturally enough, 'being' in the phrase to being and 'human' in the phrase to doing. [While thinking this may be new to you, it's not a new idea. Eckhart Tolle, for example, is very fond of it.]

What do human beings do? Well, they behave in various ways by talking, sleeping, walking, eating, working, feeling, running, thinking, having sex, and so on and on.

I find it useful to break these doings or activities into the following six kinds. This analysis is simply a practical one. The six are: living well *spiritually*, living well *emotionally*, living well *morally*, living well *intellectually*, living well *physically*, and living well *financially*. Let's agree to use the ordinary adverbs from that list in this context in a regimented way as follows:

Let's agree to use 'spiritually' to refer to disidentifying with compulsive thinking. It's less a doing than a non-doing. An awakening is an experience rather than a deliberate doing, but practicing spiritually is a kind of doing. It may be less misleading not to rank it as just another kind of doing because, when successful, it pervades the other five kinds of doings. [See the next section.]

Let's agree to use 'emotionally' to refer to feeling emotions such as anger or fear.

Let's use 'morally' to refer to interpersonal interactions such as talking or hugging. (Obviously, such interactions could also be immoral such as rape, but the point is that it's our interpersonal relationships that are the chief subject matter of ethics and political philosophy.)

Let's use 'intellectually' to refer to thinking (conceptualizing, judging). Ideally, this refers to tending our minds.

Let's use 'physically' to refer to tending our bodies, which is what we do when, for example, we sprint to exercise for improved cardiovascular fitness.

Let's use 'financially' to refer to tending to our finances by, for example, working at a job or business to increase our incomes.

This regimentation is necessary because we need to use ordinary language to communicate ideas in a more specific way than is usually necessary. We simply need to stretch ordinary language a little.

Surely these are different kinds of doings. Opening to awareness of Being is so uncommon that you may not yet have any idea what it's all about, but you should already have some understanding of Aliveness Awareness or zen meditation (zazen). Thinking is not the same kind of activity as feeling or exercising or working at a job or kissing. There are real world, familiar, experiential differences between these different kinds of doings.

So, except to satisfy logic-choppers, it would be tedious and unnecessary to specify these categories more precisely. The existence of borderline cases does not demonstrate that there are no distinctions; instead, they presuppose the distinctions.

Furthermore, within each of these six domains there are recognizable excellences. One person can be more "awake" than another. One person can be more emotional, more emotionally intense, than another. One person can be a better friend than another. One person can be a better thinker than another. One person can flourish physically more than another. One person can make and keep more money than another.

It's fruitful to break 'human' in 'human being' into five domains in order to think more clearly about what excellence is with respect to human doing.

What about 'being' in 'human being'? Is it also possible to think about what excellence is with respect to human being? The answer turns out to be grounded upon two ideas.

First, it's our being that we have in common. **We are separated by our doings; we are united in Being. Being is our essence, our whatness, our nature.** What does that mean?

The terminology here is unimportant. I stick to 'Being' for the sake of consistency. However, even just in English there are lots of other words and phrases that are used to refer to Being. Here's an incomplete list: 'Presence,' 'Aliveness,' 'God,' 'The Divine,' 'Nirvana,' 'Life-Energy,' 'Consciousness,' 'Big Mind', and 'Self' (with a capital 'S'). If you prefer, whenever you see 'Being' in a sentence here, feel free to substitute whatever other word or phrase resonates more with you.

What do these and similar words denote? I attempt to specify it more clearly in what follows.

Second, some are more fulfilled with respect to Being than others. This does not mean moral inequality. I disagree, for example, with Plato and Aristotle about this and I agree with the Stoics and Christians. *We human beings are all of equal moral value because we share the same essential nature, namely, Being.*

There is, though, a sense in which some human beings, sages, realize their true nature in a way that other human beings do not. Let's restrict using **'mastery'** and its cognates only to refer to those who are excellent in that crucial way. [That way is specified more clearly in the next section.]

The truth is that there's no wisdom, no fulfilling our potential as human beings, without mastery, without mastering life. That makes sense, doesn't it? **Someone who is wise is someone who has mastered life.** "Sages" are masters of living well.

In other words, mastery has to do with excellence as a human <u>being</u>. It's all about realizing our essential nature. It's about Being.

What, though, about doing? Let's reserve the word **'success'** and its cognates for excellence with respect to the five ordinary ways of doing just specified. It can be applied to living well in any of the nonspiritual domains of doing, which are, again, living well emotionally, living well morally, living well intellectually, living well physically, and living well financially.

Warning! Living well seems like an overwhelming or impossible task *if* you interpret it as not only mastering life by waking up to Being but also becoming successful in all those five domains. Does living well or wisely require not only mastery but excellence in the five domains of doing? If it did, there'd probably be nobody who was ever wise, who ever lived well. If you understand it that way, you may be tempted to quit immediately.

I suggest, though, that success in any of those domains is relative and should be balanced or harmonized with other important areas of life. In other words, excellence is <u>not</u> required for living well in each of the five domains of doing. Instead, what's required is only a sufficient amount of success in some of them.

Let's consider a financial example because financial success is easy to measure simply by counting someone's money. Let's suppose someone like a Bill Gates has a spectacularly successful and fast business career and becomes financially successful by the age of 30. Let's say he becomes at least a multi-millionaire. Would such a person be considered wise? Would such a person be wise?

Financial excellence, a high degree of financial success, is not the same as wisdom. Someone with lots of money is financially successful, but that hardly means that that person is automatically wise or even happy. Even though there's no need for them to be dissatisfied financially, many wealthy people are notorious for feeling very unfulfilled, very dissatisfied with their lives. In fact, since financial wealth can remove excuses, they may be more dissatisfied than the rest of us.

What you are is infinitely more important than what you have.

Some financial success may be beneficial. However, having sufficient financial success to satisfy your biologic and economic needs does not require being wealthy. As long as those needs are satisfied, you have sufficient financial success for living well.

Are you able to breathe clean air and drink clean water? Do you have clothing and shelter from inclement weather? Do you have the means to enjoy a nutritious diet? Do you have protection from criminals and other potential enemies? Are you able to interact peacefully with others? If you have sufficient wealth to enjoy those blessings right now, you already enjoy sufficient financial success for living well.

Over the last few decades there have been social scientists who have researched happiness by investigating how people report their own degrees of happiness. In general, it seems that, although poverty correlates with unhappiness, having a greater degree of financial wealth than would be considered economically middle class in developed countries does not correlate to a greater degree of satisfaction. Usually it's the peaceful countries of northern Europe such as Denmark with relatively high taxes, good government, a strong social service net that includes nearly universal day care for preschool children and universal health care, and a smaller gap between the rich and the poor that top the list of best countries to live in in terms of happiness or well-being.

Of course, you could always make more money. However, if you already enjoy a sufficient degree of financial wealth for living well, it might be wiser to work on improving your interpersonal relationships, your degree of cardiovascular fitness, or your level of understanding than to work on accumulating more money. If you are a billionaire with a troubled mind, is that degree of financial success very important at all?

So being sufficiently successful in the five domains of doing can be had at a much lower level than you may expect. Excellence in any of those domains is <u>not</u> required. Furthermore, being sufficiently successful in some of them need not take a lot of time. For example, when it comes to tending the body, it's possible to do a good job of exercising with less than an hour of exercise weekly! [See the "Introduction to Living Well Physically" section below.]

Moderation in the five domains of doing, just a sufficient degree of success in some of them, is all that may be required. Balancing or harmonizing our doings is more important than achieving excellence in any of those domains.

The answer to the next question is really important to understand: *Should there also be a balance between success and mastery?*

You might think that, once you have achieved sufficient success in each of the five domains of doing, you should then focus all your energies on mastery and that that would be the way to living well. In other words, you might think that one should balance in some such way success and mastery.

Well, frankly, no. Yes, there are two sides of our nature, namely, the domain of doing and the domain of being. Yes, there's also a sense in which they need to be balanced.

However, real wisdom comes with their integration. **Wisdom is simultaneously being well and doing well.**

Furthermore, the amount of doing required may be much, much less than you imagine. Why?

Living well is the unity of being well and doing well.

This does <u>not</u> mean, for example, focusing for some hours each day on doing well and then focusing for some other hours on being well.

In other words, *to live well is to have our doings pervaded by Being*. What? What sense does that make? How could being and doing be unified?

Let's examine that idea. What, really, is mastery? How is it possible to understand the unity of doing well and being well?

After considering the answer to that question, let's consider what we can do to achieve sufficient success in the five domains of doings, with the understanding that they are, ideally, always to be pervaded by Being.

SUGGESTIONS FOR FURTHER READING:

Bradford, D. <u>Mastery in 7 Steps</u>.
Stevenson, L., and Haberman, D. L. <u>Thirteen Theories of Human Nature</u>.

—————— ❖ ——————

Introduction to Living Well
Spiritually

Ideally, living well is constant and perpetual. Being wise, being a fully awakened sage, is not, at least in theory, a state that comes and goes. It's uninterrupted. It's not something that occurs for a while and then ceases to exist. That does happen to some who have attained some wisdom, but it doesn't happen to those who are masters, which is what I mean by using 'ideally.'

The idea expressed in the previous paragraph is, although pointing the right way, misleading. It's instructive to understand why it's misleading.

All natural languages like English are entities in Becoming, which is the domain of doing. All doings require time. They have beginnings, middles, and endings. The word 'Becoming' is a gerund, a verbal noun. Verbs are action words. Actions, doings, are temporal. Becoming is temporal.

Insofar as our lives have, like stories, beginnings, middles, and endings, they are temporal. However, as strange as it may initially seem, *thinking of our lives as solely temporal is radically misleading.* Understanding why is really the topic of this section.

"Forms" (objects; whatever can be singled out for our attention, whether or not they are real or taken to be real) are contents in Becoming. When you hammer a nail, the hammer, the nail, and the hammering are all entities (existences, real forms). Actually, there are also nonentities (unreal forms) in Becoming, too, such as the objects of nonveridical perceptions like the puddle on the highway I saw while driving last summer that turned out to be a mirage or the green blob in my dream last night that threatened to envelop me.

However, Being is nontemporal (eternal, outside time, timeless). Actually, since Being is beyond all conceptualization, it's also beyond the temporal/nontemporal distinction. How could words from natural languages possibly describe Being? Being is also formless; there are no forms in Being. Actually, again, since Being is beyond all conceptualization, it's also beyond the form/no-form distinction. Conceptualizations (thoughts, judgments) about Being are impossible. There's no way to describe Being other than the negative way of saying that it's unlike Becoming. It has no content.

Notice that 'Being' with a capital 'B' denotes the timeless, formless realm and 'being' with a small 'b' denotes a form.

Remember that concepts are principles of classification (discrimination, sorting, categorization, division). They are objects that are themselves used to sort other objects. Again, if you are able to classify some shirts as red and others as not-red, you have the concept redness. Since there are no objects in Being whatsoever, there are no contents in Being, including concepts.

This is why traditional Buddhist terms for Being are often translated as 'Emptiness.' That translation, though, is misleading and has caused a lot of confusion such as thinking of Buddhism as a nihilism. It's much better to call Being something like 'the fecund void,' which seems to denote a contradiction. Good! Contradictory phrases like 'the round square' supposedly denote logically impossible objects that cannot be thought (because a shape cannot be both circular and non-circular simultaneously). Nor can Being be singled out any more than the round square. There's no use trying to conceptualize Being.

Claiming that living well is, ideally, constant and perpetual is claiming that living well is temporal. Because we ordinarily restrict ourselves to thinking or talking about Becoming, there's nothing necessarily wrong with claiming that living well is constant and perpetual.

However, insofar as living well involves opening to (having direct nonconceptual awareness of, participating in) Being, that claim is misleading because there's nothing constant or perpetual about Being. Don't think of Being as something that exists at all times; instead, Being is wholly outside time. It's easier to think and talk that way, but, again, since Being is beyond all conceptual distinctions such as the temporal/nontemporal distinction it's also misleading to call it nontemporal.

Because as human beings we are able to open to or participate in both Becoming and Being and because living well involves our whole being and not just part of it, it's misleading to think of living well just as being temporal. Instead, it requires opening to the eternal, which is beyond anything temporal. That explains why, although it's a point that applies in Becoming, claiming that living well is perpetual and constant is misleading.

Living well requires opening to Being. There can be no living well without nonconceptual awareness of Being; in other words, the content of spirituality is being in Being. Opening to Being is what living well spiritually is all about.

It's important not to confuse the meaning of 'spiritual' with the meaning of 'religious.' If we agree that being religious involves accepting some creed or other, then, other than accidentally, being religious has nothing to do with spirituality. This is not, of course, to deny that some people who accept religious creeds, including monotheistic creeds, are also spiritual. That can happen. Some are. It seems to me, for example, that people like Meister Eckhart and Thomas Keating are both spiritual and religious.

The critical proposition to understand in this context is that religious creeds without spirituality are nothing but ideologies (conceptual hierarchies or frameworks). If you accept a religious creed, you'll naturally use its concepts to understand spiritual or waking experiences. The point, though, is that that's not necessary. It's the awakening experience (waking, <u>kensho</u>, spiritual experience, <u>satori</u>) that's important, not its conceptual interpretation. Nonreligious interpretations may be just as —or more – effective in explaining spiritual experiences even though it's impossible for there to be any conceptual understanding of Being.

How, then, do we apprehend Being if we cannot do so conceptually? Well, do you expect here a conceptual description of the direct apprehension of Being? Not only won't you find it here, you won't find it anywhere.

Being can be experienced directly and nonconceptually. In fact, without doing that it's impossible to live well. Why? Without a balance or interpenetration between Becoming and Being, there's only a one-sidedness or radical imbalance that makes living well impossible. After all, since everything in Becoming is transitory, since nothing abides in Becoming, fulfillment in Becoming can only be transitory. Transitory fulfillment is not genuine fulfillment.

Living well or wisely is simultaneously being well and doing well.

The realm of Becoming is the realm of incessant flux, everlasting impermanence. There's no genuine stillness. The realm of Being is the realm of genuine stillness. There is no flux, no impermanence. How, then, could there be an opening between or interpenetration of the two realms? How could there be unity between flux and stillness?

Experiencing that unity is living well spiritually. The initial problem is understanding what that means. Since Being cannot be conceptualized, there can be no conceptual understanding of living well. Spiritual teachers for millennia have pointed out that trying to conceptualize Being is a grave mistake. It's a futile, impossible task.

At best, words and concepts can only be used to point in the direction of realizing the union of Becoming and Being.

Perhaps a familiar kind of analogy may help here. Please think of a peak performance. Recall your mastering some skill or other. It might have been learning to walk or talk or read. It might have been learning how to play a musical instrument such as the piano or French horn. It might have been learning some sport-specific skill like firing a slap shot in hockey or making a free throw in basketball. It might have been learning some game such as chess or go. It might have been learning some fun skill like juggling, doing card tricks, or dancing.

Please recall in detail how you learned to master it. Think back to when you were a mere beginner. You began with a desire to acquire the skill. You may have realized that you needed other, more advanced people to emulate, because you initially needed to understand what to do. For example, suppose that you have mastered playing the French horn. What happened the first time someone handed you one? Did you have any idea what to do with it? Could you even make a sound with it? You certainly had no idea how to make it play a musical tune.

You had a goal that you wanted to achieve, namely, for whatever reason you wanted to learn how to play the French horn well. Given access to a French horn, you needed a teacher. (These days, you might be able to go on YouTube and find some suitable instructions for beginners.) With the help of your teacher, you began to drill and practice regularly.

Initially, you had to think hard about everything you were doing such as your breathing, your body positioning, your lips, your fingering, the notes, and the rhythm. That probably required learning musical theory and how to read music. You learned what worked and what didn't work. You made lots and lots of mistakes and tried to learn from them. You persisted. You took obstacles as opportunities to learn more. If you really did become a master French horn player, you probably practiced for at least an hour or two every day for quite a few years.

Perhaps, at first, practicing was very frustrating. It all seemed very, very difficult. Being determined, though, you kept at it. Eventually, you could make sounds and then even pleasing sounds. Eventually, you could make music. You began to enjoy practice sessions, even when there seemed to be no progress. You focused attention on practicing and practiced as well as you were able to practice as frequently as you were able to practice.

One day when you were playing your teacher exclaimed, "That's it!" What's it? You didn't think that you were doing anything differently from what you'd done dozens or hundreds or thousands of times before. Still, something was different. You were playing with quality or excellence.

What happened, you realized later, was that you were no longer trying to play that piece of music. Instead, you had become the playing of the music! All separateness had disappeared including, importantly, egocentricity or the self/nonself distinction.

As you continued to practice every day, there was eventually a second "Zen moment." Then a third. They may have stopped coming for a while, but you kept practicing and, eventually, they began to happen more and more frequently while you were playing. Those are the **moments of mastery.** They mark the master's path.

Didn't it work something like that when you mastered whatever it was that you mastered? That's an example of the unity of being and doing. Yes, the masterful playing of the piece took time but, during it, you wholly lacked time consciousness.

As Plotinus remarks at this point in the dialectic, you either understand the kinds of peak experiences I'm referring to or you don't. If you do, you don't need more examples. If you don't, more examples won't help.

Those are moments of pure joy wholly without egocentricity or thought. They are experiences in which the whole world seems perfect. In that sense, they are moments of unadulterated Being or utter stillness even though they are also moments of doing (activity, actions, behaviors).

It initially seems a strange claim but the real purpose of mastering the French horn is not mastering the French horn. **The real purpose of mastering any skill is mastering life**, experiencing the union of Being and Becoming. It's sometimes summed up by saying, "Let go and let Buddha." With mastery may come a glimpse of its most important benefit, namely, awakening beyond Becoming.

However, although with continued, focused practice of the right kind, limited or restricted experiences become less limited or restricted, the problem of beginning the route to mastery by starting with such specific kinds of doings as mastering a musical instrument is that they don't extend throughout other experiences. Does a master of the French horn live any better than the rest of us when he or she is not playing a French horn? No. Furthermore, a master of the French horn is likely to be too attached to playing a French horn because it has become so enjoyable. By way of contrast, sages are detached from any particular kind of experience. As Meister Eckhart puts it, the greatest virtue is detachment because it's what makes all the other virtues possible.

This is why it's preferable to work on purifying (disciplining, training) the mind directly by some classic meditative practice such as Aliveness Awareness or zazen than it is to focus too much on becoming successful in any of the five usual domains of doing. One way to express this is to state that thoughts are noise and it's easier to extend the stillness experienced in a meditative practice to any domains of doing than it is to extend excellence achieved in one of those domains of doing to other domains.

We all find it very easy to understand ourselves as temporal beings. We all are attached to our own stories. We relish telling each other about them. We identify with our pasts and spend a lot of time trying to create even better futures for ourselves. We may practice self-talk such as, "Hey, I may not be fulfilled or satisfied in the present moment, but I'm going to do whatever it takes so that my story has a really happy ending!" We may post notes on the bathroom mirror or refrigerator as reminders.

The fundamental problem about living well is that our ordinary understanding is radically incomplete. To begin to grasp this, ask yourself, "If I abstract from my past and my future, who am I?" Detach from all memories about your life so far. Detach from all hopes and fears about your life to come. Right now, who are you?

What if time isn't ultimately real? That's a great question! It's similar to particle physicists asking, *What if space isn't ultimately real?* These are wonderful questions that point beyond our present conceptual understanding.

Who has moments of mastery? Well, perhaps nobody! Why assume that experiences must be had by persons? Introspect a la the Buddha or David Hume. Do you find a person in there at all? *What would it even be like to find one?*

Descartes was the father of modern western philosophy. The bedrock of his fundamental thinking was cogito ergo sum ("I think therefore I am"). He grounded his fundamental thinking on that piece of knowledge. In a sense, he was correct: the existence of consciousness or awareness is indubitable (because doubt itself require consciousness).

In another sense, though, he was incorrect. As Nietzsche argued, the I (the ego/I, the self, the so-called small self) is dubitable. Descartes, like Aristotle, assumes that there must be a person who has the consciousness. That's linguistically true in the sense that 'I think' is a well-formed sentence. What, though, exactly does the 'I' denote?

The issue here is the fundamental divide between substance ontologies and nonsubstance ontologies. If we remove or abstract from an individual's qualities, either something is left or nothing is left, either there's an ontological surd or there isn't. Is it possible even to think of a qualityless individual? How could something with no qualities even be thought? It can't, which is why substance ontologies like those of Aristotle and Descartes are wrong-headed. [I've discussed this more extensively in other writings.]

Moments of mastery require detachment from conceptualizing (thinking, judging). They **require alert awareness without conceptualizing**, which is why it's often claimed that they require "no-thought." This is why it's impossible to think one's way to mastery.

Conceptualizing is doing. Thinking is a kind of activity. Understanding something new is often hard work. As a kind of doing, it's absent from Being. If there is thought, there cannot be apprehension of Being. Again, there are neither individuals nor qualities in Being; there's nothing there to think.

One might claim that there are no divisions in Being. Being is a whole; it's not part of a whole. However, even that's misleading. Why? Being is "beyond" all concepts and conceptualizations and the part/whole distinction, though often very useful in Becoming, is just another concept.

Again, to think (conceptualize, judge) is to divide. To think that this is a red shirt, is to sort this shirt into a category of having a quality that not all objects have. This means that, from a logical point of view, all thoughts (conceptualizations, judgments) are partial. They cannot not be partial, because their whole purpose is to divide or separate or break down their subject matter in an attempt to render it more intelligible.

What this entails with respect to Becoming is that, at best, a thought can only be a partial truth. No thought captures the whole truth. This is why **fanatics** or true believers, who are the opposite of philosophers, are always fools. Attachment to any thought is foolish in the sense that no thought can be wholly true.

What this entails with respect to Being is that, as indivisible and "beyond" all conceptualizations, it cannot be thought. This is an important mistake that many excellent thinkers, including **philosophers**, make. They think that they can think their way to wisdom without grasping that wisdom requires opening to Being via no-thought. By attaching themselves to thinking, they perpetually block their own apprehension of Being.

Living well requires both some good thinking in Becoming as well as nonconceptual awareness of Being. Many people seem to be either wholly unaware of Being or unaware of how to experience it directly (in other words, nonconceptually).

It's simple to experience Being: just drop all thoughts. That's it! Easy, no. Simple, yes.

Fortunately, you already have two valuable advantages over those people. First, you now understand the theoretical claim that practicing no-thought to the point of mastery is what is required. Second, at least if you have begun practicing either Aliveness Awareness or zazen as I recommended in *Stress Reduction Wizardry* (or have some other effective spiritual or meditative practice or yoga), you are using a practical way to living well that's been proven to work for other people for millennia.

Guess what? **The way to experience Being is simply to drop all thought**. It's instantaneous. What's difficult for nearly everyone is practicing sufficiently so that no-thought becomes a live option.

Thoughts are heavy; they are like a weight we carry around. We do all kinds of things to try to relieve that burden. We use alcohol or other psychoactive drugs. We engage in dangerous sports like auto or motorcycle racing. We engage in dangerous activities like hang-gliding, bridge-jumping, or mountain climbing. Why? Why risk life and limb? It's because the intense focus they can stimulate allows us to escape temporarily from heavy thoughts.

There's another relief available, however, that's not dangerous. Mastering a meditative (spiritual, yogic) practice is normally required for breaking thought addiction, which is our fundamental problem when it comes to living well. Obviously, it's impossible to think one's way out of compulsive "thoughting" (to use Roshi Kapleau's term). Nearly everyone has to practice no-thought well to master no-thought, which is opening to Being.

Reading and hearing talks and so on can help you improve your understanding. That's important work. However, if you were to spend too much time doing that and too little time practicing, you'll fail to live well because you'll fail to open to Being. Without opening to Being, you'll remain radically incomplete or out of balance, which is not the way to wisdom. As my spiritual teacher [Bodhin Kjolhede, Roshi] told me when I first began practicing a quarter of a century ago, *if reading helps you to practice, read; if it doesn't, don't.*

The biggest problem with respect to having any kind of formal practice such as Aliveness Awareness or zazen is extending the stillness that may be generated. If all one does is to practice well for an hour or two daily and then ignores stillness for the other 22 or 23 hours of that day, sagehood will remain elusive.

"Mini-meditations" are a classic solution. Typically, there are repetitive tasks in our daily lives such as waking up in the morning, answering the phone, driving a car, washing the dishes, brushing our teeth, and so on. Usually, we pay no attention to them because we are busy thinking about supposedly more important things.

There is nothing more important than what's going on right now. Why? There is no other time to live. The past no longer exists; the future does not yet exist. If you miss life in this moment because you are separated from it in thought, you are missing life.

Unlike the rest of us, sages don't miss life. It's impossible to live well if you miss life.

Traditionally, gathas are used to focus our attention on the present moment. They are little sayings that one can use before routine tasks. [See Thich Nhat Hanh's book in the Suggestions for Further Reading section at the end of this section if you'd like some examples. I've used his waking up gatha before getting out of bed every morning for over twenty years.] The idea of using them is to pay attention to whatever we are doing. For example, every time you get into a car to drive it, sit motionless for a little while until you begin to feel the aliveness in your hands or feet and then start the car.

Although practicing is critical in the sense that there's no living well without it, it does not follow that there are no spontaneous breakthroughs to Being. There are. It's just that without a spiritual practice to extend them, they won't have any lasting beneficial effects.

If you are alert for them, it's possible to extend them temporally. If you have no clue what they are or their value, you'll skip right past them and ignore them. It may help you to notice them by comparing and contrasting our everyday consciousness of Becoming with consciousness of Being after awakening experiences.

As many spiritual teachers have said, the most important initial obstruction there is to living well is attachment to the thought that our everyday consciousness of Becoming provides a true account of reality. It doesn't. Assuming that our ordinary perceptions are accurate and reveal what really is is just an extreme form of what philosophers call "naïve realism."

In modern western philosophy, it was Kant who opened the door to realizing that our everyday perceptions are radically infected by our concepts, the structure of our minds. Attachments to the ordinary way of understanding that we grew up with distorts what we take reality to be. The real world is different from the way we ordinarily take it to be.

When we wake up in the morning, we naturally realize that whatever we took to be reality in our dreams wasn't correct. Similarly, when we wake up spiritually, we naturally realize that whatever we took to be reality in our everyday perception of Becoming wasn't correct.

What is the everyday perception of Becoming that we wake up *from*?

That **normal state** of everyday consciousness (awareness) is one of anxiety, generalized fear. We take ourselves to be separate, isolated, and alone, which is a source of great discontent and dissatisfaction. We find ourselves in a dead or inanimate world that is utterly meaningless. Whatever of value we are or do is impermanent. Our degree of mental health is sub-optimal. We never take ourselves to be enjoying perpetual well-being. We take ourselves to be bound by time and, since we are dissatisfied, we hope for future fulfillment while having to admit that the future also will contain our deaths, which will wholly undermine whatever we value. Such is the human condition.

Upon examination, we may come to realize that we are tightly bound to our egos, our self-concepts. There is a clear boundary between ourselves and everything else. Our egocentric perspectives are relative to us. Our most common thoughts involve the meanings of "I," "myself," and "me."

Unawakened consciousness of manifested Becoming is **madness** (dysfunctional, pathological). The world seems fragmented, which creates a neediness for identity or belonging, in other words, for acceptance and approval from others. Events seem random and without real value, which creates a neediness not only for frequent diversions but also for gaining something else to make us feel better. We feel disconnected from ourselves and from others. Our ego's create unrelenting chatter that the deluded identify with their real selves. We take ourselves to have personal agency without the means to make good decisions, which generates a perpetual conflict between wanting to be proud of and responsible for our lives and realizing that all our decisions are like shots into the dark. Our continued existence makes no important difference one way or the other. This world, to echo Sophocles, sounds an eternal note of sadness. It's not difficult to understand why spiritual teachers often state that a normal self has a "lower" state of consciousness.

To have an awakening or mystical experience is to have conceptually-unfiltered apprehension of Being. We take ourselves to be connected to everything else; all things are at one. We find ourselves in a living or animate world that seems wholly pervaded by a great spirit. Our degree of mental health is optimal or, even, optimific. We take reality to be benevolent and harmonious. It radiates meaningfulness and well-being. We are content and peaceful to such a degree that we experience abiding bliss, ecstasy, and joy.

Upon examination, we come to realize that there's been a shift in the attachments that make up the structure of our egos. The overdeveloped egoic structure characteristic of people from "advanced" cultures has shifted. The more complete the shift, the more consciousness is unburdened by ego. The boundary between ourselves and everything else has (partially or wholly) dissolved; we experience a refreshing and light egolessness. We feel love for everything else for the simple reason that we take ourselves ultimately to be everything else; in other words, the life force that creates them also created us so that we share the same essence (Being). We realize an identity with that which is non-material and eternal, in other words, we realize that, essentially, we are indestructible. The intensity of a genuine waking experience is completed by a sense of serenity.

Awakened consciousness of unmanifested Being is **sanity**. The world seems whole. All seems as it should be, which undermines all obstructions to bliss. There is no sense that we need to adopt some identity to inject life with meaning. There's self-sufficiency without any need for acceptance and approval from others. There's a feeling of completeness that undermines any urge to gain something that will somehow complete ourselves. There's no need any more to fill awareness with incessant chatter. There's a more intense apprehension of reality that provides a powerful sense of serenity and well-being. This is an abiding joy rather than the joy of a normal self that fluctuates with sorrow. There's a powerful stillness that generates real love and compassion. We feel ourselves so connected to others that we identify with them. Our acts of service, then, are Self-serving rather than self-serving. There's a feeling that they are not really "our" acts at all; rather, it's as if a pervading benevolent force is acting through us. The world is alive and the right place for us to be. We feel that we are experiencing the world rather than just trying to conceptualize it. It's not difficult to understand why spiritual teachers often state that those who enjoy awakened experiences enjoy a "higher" state of consciousness.

One could say that a normal self experiences ordinary consciousness in which there is a subject/object duality. In other words, the subject is different from its object. For example, think of the judgment "I see the tree." 'I' denotes the subject; 'the tree' denotes the object. By way of contrast, an awakened self has pure consciousness in which there is unity of subject and object. Being is pure consciousness. Its purity is its emptiness. Instead of the duality of the previous sample judgment, there's just "tree-awareness" in which unity replaces separation. This is why some spiritual teachers claim that the goal of meditation is the unity that occurs when all differences between subject and object dissolve. Others state that both subject and object fall away, just as self consciousness and consciously trying both drop away in a peak performance. Instead of identification with the subject who is performing, there is disidentification with the performing subject, which just leaves the whole performance itself.

The most important feature of awakening experiences is that they engender a feeling of timelessness. At least in the Buddhist tradition, there's a lot of talk about the "is-ness" of things. It's not just that awakened perceptions have a vivid intensity that unawakened perceptions lack (because ordinary ones are deadened by thoughts), but also that they have a "now-ness." Life in the present moment is wholly engaging, so engaging that past and future become meaningless. In other words, the importance of time evaporates. Life only occurs now. Merely thinking that thought is easy and everyone agrees abstractly. Realizing that life only occurs in the endless now, however, is the sine qua non of awakening experiences.

How does the shift from a normal self to an awakened self happen? Very occasionally, there may be people for whom the higher state of consciousness is natural. Sometimes the shift happens quickly as a result of immense suffering. Typically, though, the shift happens gradually, over a period of years and it's stimulated by spiritual practices such as meditation. The shift itself may be temporary or permanent.

Waking experiences are not only universal in different human cultures, but they are also transformative when they are permanent. They do, though, come in different intensities. More mild waking experiences are characteristic of childhood and so-called "primitive" peoples; more intense waking experiences are typically the result of mastering a spiritual practice, although they can also be caused by great suffering.

Again, the analogy to peak performances can be helpful in understanding waking experiences. As in the example of mastering the French horn, moments of mastery can be set up by a lot of deliberate, focused practicing. **Moments of mastery are actually consciousness unbound by thought.** They involve a different experience of time, namely, one without past or future. They are not only blissful and beautiful, but they involve a more intense reality than the reality revealed by our normal state of everyday consciousness.

Waking up changes everything and nothing. The key to understanding this is to understand the fundamental importance of identity and existential judgments in the constitution of our surrealities. *What is real is what is multiply identifiable.* A material identity judgment has the logical form *x is y* and asserts that two apparently different forms (objects) are one entity (existent). In other words, an entity (existent) may be singled out in two or more ways. For example, this piece of paper that I'm touching is the same piece of paper that I'm seeing. [I've written in multiple places about this, but the best account is in Butchvarov's Being Qua Being.] The unawakened do not identify with supposedly other objects, whereas the awakened do. To use John Muir's examples, does the sun shine on you and the river flow past you, or does the sun shine in you and the river flow through you?

Lots of people, especially those attached to metaphysical materialism, write off waking experiences as being caused by, for example, unusual chemistry in the brain. Anyone who advocates that interpretation is just someone (perhaps terminally) attached to an ideology.

If you permit me a personal story, I first realized that this might be the case in a philosophy of religion course that I took as an undergraduate. My old professor, who died about a year later, made the point in class one day that mystics were never swayed by rational arguments. It was obvious to them that their experience of reality was better than the reality revealed by our normal state of everyday consciousness.

If you doubt that, and there's no reason why you shouldn't, find out for yourself. How? Excellent question!

It's true that homeostatic disruptions such as fasting, sleep deprivation, ingesting certain drugs, and so on can sometimes stimulate waking experiences. However, at best, such experiences provide glimpses of Being. They do not provide permanent awakening and, even if they could, that would be very dangerous. [In case you are wondering, I myself have experienced more than one temporary awakening experience.]

It's also true that severe suffering can cause a waking experience. For example, Eckhart Tolle may be the best as well as most popular spiritual teacher of our era and that's how he woke up. Deliberately seeking severe suffering in the hopes that it will stimulate a waking experience rather than, say, suicide seems to me a very unpalatable alternative.

According to all spiritual teachers, waking up is the greatest human experience. **Waking up is our most important task.**

Fortunately, there's a way to do it that is not dangerous, namely, mastering some spiritual practice or other such as Aliveness Awareness or zazen. Every experience is an opportunity for awakening. Furthermore, all of us are able to do it; it does not require us to be spiritual geniuses like the Buddha,

Jesus, Plotinus, Saint Francis, Meister Eckhart, or Ramana Maharshi.

We weren't born with our egoic structures; we learned them. Therefore, at least in theory, we are able to unlearn them in the sense that we are able to let them go.

On the other hand, awakening experiences can be very confusing, frustrating, and even debilitating when they occur suddenly without a coherent conceptual framework for understanding them. When they are the result of practicing, though, they feel very natural even though they are initially extraordinary.

An important danger of talking about normal and awakened states of consciousness is that, as always, conceptualizing them deadens them. Thinking abstractly may create the false impression that, for example, being awake isn't an evolving process. No, **wakefulness evolves**. For example, if an initial awakening experience occurs after years of focused spiritual practice, it can easily take another decade before its ramifications are integrated throughout someone's life.

Strictly speaking, it's not persons who are awakened or not. It's experiences. It's often easier to think or talk as if persons were awake or not, but that's misleading.

There is no single, clear criterion for dividing normal from awakened states of consciousness. If it helps, think of states of consciousness as being on a continuum. In the Zen tradition of koan training, for example, masters judge their students on whether or not they have passed a koan, but a passing evaluation for some masters is different from a passing evaluation from other masters. [Would you like to rate yourself using a psychological wakefulness inventory? If so, there's one near the end of S. Taylor's The Leap.]

Permit me to emphasize that the sustained effort required to wake up is, although available to everyone, simply too difficult for most people. It requires too much ethical regulation, puri-fication, focus, self-discipline, renunciation, intense effort, and service. Given the infrequency with which sages occur among us, this may not be surprising.

"Spiritual materialism" is a serious obstacle for many who undertake a spiritual practice. It's the idea that, for example, I have something important to gain by becoming a sage. In other words, it's an egocentric motivation. Actually, as the practice proceeds, this motivation tends to dissolve. What happens is that the everyday ego is transcended and transformed. This, too, may not be surprising. If you have ever met a sage, you'll have met someone who is genuinely humble and egocentric in such a different and better way that he or she may seem wholly nonegocentric.

However, this does not automatically entail that awaken-ing experiences, even when intensified and sustained by spiri-tual practice, automatically entail ethical behavior. They don't. Sometimes, even though they are less likely to do so than the rest of us, even sages behave immorally. What should happen (and usually does happen) is that moral behavior is a precondi-tion of, or accompaniment to, spiritual training.

Also, don't assume that sages have no challenges in life. They do. The key difference is only that, unlike the rest of us, they don't automatically turn challenges into problems.

What follows are six suggestions that, if followed, will not only decrease stress and dissatisfaction but also will move you toward lasting wakefulness. [I've found S. Taylor's books quite helpful about this and other topics in this section.]

First, the most important single thing we can do is to med-itate. This has been known for at least the last two-and-one-half millennia. As the Buddha said, **"There can be no med-itation for those who are not wise, and no wisdom for those who do not meditate"** [from The Dhammapada].

So be as kind as possible to yourself and others as well as to the earth and universe by practicing meditation daily. There are many different kinds of meditation that work. If Aliveness Awareness or zazen don't happen to work well for you, find another kind that will, perhaps a moving meditation such as t'ai chi.

I recommend a minimum of two sessions daily of 20 or 30 minutes, preferably at the beginning of the day and at the end of the day.

Second, use mini-meditations or gathas to help you pay attention to the present moment multiple times daily. Instead of being incessantly lost in thoughts, frequently practice dropping them. Practice frequently throughout the day paying attention to now. If you do, you'll quickly find that the quality of your experiences will increase.

Third, practice moderation in the sense of the Buddha's middle way between asceticism and indulgence. Recognize cravings and desires and tame them. There are all kinds of things we may want such as food, sex, alcohol and other drugs, sensory stimulation, possessions, success in any of the five domains of doing, status, fame, power, fortune, and so on. Remember K.I.S.S.: keep it simple, stupid.

Fourth, consider deliberately breaking psychological attachments whenever you notice them. No, you do not need to sell your dream house if you happen to be living in it. You could, but it's not necessary. The idea is to remind yourself that what matters is abiding satisfaction and contentment, and it's not necessary to own possessions to live well. Owning possessions is typically troublesome and time-consuming, which is why many spiritual traditions recommend against it.

One way to break attachments is to give them up temporarily. For example, if your house is cool in the summer, warm in the winter, and has indoor plumbing like showers and toilets with hot and cold running water, take a tent into the bush regularly and give up all those comforts for a week or so. You'll not only appreciate them more when you return home, but you'll also realize that they are not necessary for living well.

Be careful, though, when practicing psychological detachment not simply to replace one attachment with another. The ego is a wily opponent ever ready to reappear. This is an important reason why having a master's personal guidance is extremely helpful.

Fifth, regularly get away into silent solitude without doing more than the minimum required for survival. **Silence is the language of Being**. All noise comes from Becoming. Perhaps the biggest distractions in most of our lives are other people, which is why periods of solitude are critical. Be still and silent alone.

Is there a monastery or nunnery near you that would allow you to live there for a few days very inexpensively? [There's one right in my county.] Spending a weekend there or a week may be much more beneficial than you initially imagine.

Similarly, there are spiritual retreats available all over the world. I have elsewhere mentioned the benefits of a week-long sesshin [zen retreat], although they can be very painful and are too intense for many people.

Sixth, find ways to be of service to others. The volunteer's creed is that *it's impossible to give more than you receive.*

What kinds of lives do sages live? Lives of selfless service. Because they are the least egotistical of all people, sages are the greatest lovers. Find what would be best for others and help them improve their lives.

Permit me to give Gandhi the last words in this section: "The best way to find yourself is to lose yourself in the service of others."

SUGGESTIONS FOR FURTHER READING

Abram, D. The Spell of the Sensuous

Begley, S. Train Your Mind Change Your Brain

Bradford, D. Are You Living Without Purpose?

Csikszentmihalyi, M. Flow

Eckhart, M. Selected Writings. Oliver Davies, ed.

Emerson, R. W. Essays

Hanh, Thich Nhat. Present Moment Wonderful Moment

Happold, F.C. Mysticism

Herrigel, E. Zen in the Art of Archery

Huntington, C. W., & Wangchen, G. N. The Emptiness of
   Emptiness

Kapleau, P. The Three Pillars of Zen

Katie, B. Loving What Is

Lao, Tzu. Tao Te Ching. Jonathan Star, ed.

Loori, J. D. Riding the Ox Home

Nagarguna. The Fundamental Wisdom of the Middle Way.
   Jay L. Garfield, ed.

Osho. Meditation

Scharfstein, B. Mystical Experience

Schucman, H. A Course in Miracles

Suizuki, S. Zen Mind Beginner's Mind

Taylor, S. The Leap

Taylor, S. Waking from Sleep

The Buddha. Basic Teachings of the Buddha. G. Wallis, ed.

The Buddha. In the Buddha's Words. Bhikkhu Bodhi, ed.

Thoreau, H. D. On Walden Pond

Tolle, E. A New Earth

Tolle, E. The Power of Now

Unknown. <u>The Bhagavad Gita</u>. E. Easwaran, tr.
Unknown. <u>The Upanishads</u>. E. Easwaran, tr.
Westerhoff, J. <u>Nagarjuna's Madhyamaka</u>
Whitman, W. <u>Song of Myself</u>

Introduction to Living Well
Emotionally

Confusion about emotions (passions) is rampant. The result is not surprising: few people flourish emotionally. Since this is unnecessary, it's also sad.

My claim is *that it's possible for you to do better emotionally for the rest of your life. Furthermore, you don't have to become a sage to do it.* (In case you haven't yet read the previous section "Introduction to Living Well Spiritually," a sage is someone who enjoys lasting spiritual wakefulness.)

Please ask, 'How may I live better emotionally from now on?' I argue briefly for my answer to that question in this section.

If you suffer from immature ideas about emotions, that question itself will seem odd to you. The chief of those ideas is the myth of passivity. The myth of emotional passivity is the idea that we are not responsible for our emotions. Instead, like weather fronts, when they happen, emotions just wash over us and, so, we are powerless to do anything about them.

Ordinary language reflects and directs ordinary thinking. The myth of passivity is engrained in ordinary language. There's talk, for example, about being *paralyzed* by fear as if we were quadriplegics, *distracted* by anger as if someone in the next room were playing music so loudly that it was annoying, *driven* by revenge as if being poked by a cattle prod, *taken* by surprise as if kidnapped, and so on.

A belief is a thought (conceptualization, judgment) we attach to or accept. Since thoughts are doings, so are beliefs. If you believe something, own it. It's yours. Accept responsibility for it.

Thoughts are inherently partial, in other words, never wholly true because they are conceptualizations that require the use of concepts, which are principles of separation. In other words, all thoughts are perspectival.

Since all thoughts are perspectival and since beliefs are kinds of thoughts, it follows that all beliefs are perspectival. This is why we should all be humble when it comes to our beliefs and always willing to improve them (instead of fanatically attaching to them). Of course, many people lack the courage to be open-minded and curious, which is the courage of a philosopher.

Why is this relevant?

It's because emotions are kinds of beliefs. **Emotions are relatively intense evaluative judgments.**

To claim that they are "relatively intense" is to claim that they are beliefs accompanied by physiological (bodily, physical) changes. We are so attached to them that our bodies as well as our minds are affected by them. This explains why simply thinking about emotions can intensify them and explains why, the more intense they are, the easier it becomes to focus on them. Thus, *a vicious cycle of thoughts and corresponding emotions can occur*. Since thoughts are central to experiencing an emotion, the more we think about the relevant situation the more intense that emotion becomes and the more intense that emotion becomes the more our attention narrows to focus even more exclusively on that situation.

It also explains why we cannot simply think our way out of them. You've undoubtedly tried *shoulding* on intense unwanted emotions (for example, "I shouldn't be disgusted by that" or "I shouldn't be grief-stricken about her death") to no avail.

In fact [as I have argued in print in multiple places], the two extreme ordinary methods for dealing with unwanted emotions don't work well. The first is *ignoring*, which fails miserably for the simple reason that, since you have to be aware of something to ignore it, awareness of the unwanted emotion is sustained. The second is *venting*, acting out emotionally like a child, which typically perpetuates and often even strengthens an emotion. Some people try deliberately to channel emotional energies by venting such as when a football player psyches up before a game to generate hatred of the other team, but the long-term effects of doing that are destructive.

Emotions are disruptive. They always undermine serenity. This is why we never associate sagehood with emotionality. Do sages feel emotions? Yes. Typically, though, they feel them with greatly decreased intensity and, more importantly, they are able to use the spiritual practice they've mastered to decrease their duration as well as their intensity significantly. They are, therefore, freer from emotional slavery than the rest of us.

Moods are generalized emotions. In other words, they may not be about some particular form. Moods and emotions are on a continuum; they blend into each other. Sages are the least moody people you'll ever meet. Typically, they are always even-keeled and upbeat.

Descriptive judgments describe what is the case. If I were to ask you what we are listening to and you answered, "The third movement of Beethoven's 9th Symphony," your answer expressed a descriptive judgment. If I were then to state, "I like it," that answer would express an evaluative judgment. Typically, emotions require almost instantaneous appraisals of good or bad, liking or disliking.

There's no such thing as a complete list of emotions (although Solomon's list in his <u>The Passions</u> is very complete). Instead, it's better to follow Ekman in <u>Emotions Revealed</u> and divide all emotions into one of seven genera, namely, *sadness, anger, surprise, fear, disgust, contempt,* and *happiness.*

Does something immediately strike you about that list? Please look at it again.

Notice that of the seven genera only one is positive; six of the seven kinds are negative.

This should not really be surprising. After all, at least until we break the habit, we spend our days incessantly thinking. In general, what do we think about? Our problems. We all have challenges, but what those of us who are foolish do is to think about them continually and turn them into problems. Why don't we think about our successes instead? What's there to think about? Successes are like solved puzzles; there's nothing more to do with them. Problems are like unsolved puzzles that are easy to dwell on.

Ekman defines emotions as processes that require distinctive automatic appraisals in which we (i) "sense something important to our welfare is occurring" accompanied by (ii) "physiological changes and emotional behaviors" that begin to address their reality.

Emotions occur naturally. Mother Nature gave us the ability to feel emotions, which really means that they have survival value. Obviously, if six times out of seven we react quickly to situations that threaten our welfare, we are more likely to survive and thrive than otherwise. If I notice that I accidentally stepped too near a puff adder and jump back without taking the time to think about the situation or decide what to do about it, I'm more likely to survive than if I had lacked the ability to experience fear.

Normally emotional people are able to relate to other people in three relevant ways. *Cognitive empathy* is recognizing what someone else is feeling. *Emotional empathy* is feeling what someone else is feeling. *Compassionate empathy* is desiring to help someone else deal with an emotional difficulty.

At least cognitive empathy and compassionate empathy are components of flourishing emotionally. Sages almost always have both abilities. (Sociopaths have neither.) Notice, though, that both require us to get beyond ourselves, which really means getting over ourselves. This requires emotional maturity. Be suspicious of people who cannot genuinely laugh at themselves.

By way of contrast, sometimes emotionally immature people believe in the myth of innocence, which is the idea that, prior to critical reflection about emotions, they are always valuable because they are free, natural, and spontaneous. Balderdash! That's mere irresponsibility. It elevates childish emotions to the point of worshipping them (as some Romantics were inclined to do).

False belief in the myth of innocence often goes with false belief in the myth of irrationality, which is the myth that emotions are irrational. No, they are never irrational. Examine your own life and ask, "Have I ever been intensely emotional whenever there was no reason to be emotional?" Perhaps, for example, you were very emotional when your lover died or dumped you. Well, wasn't that death or break-up the reason for your emotion?

We are emotional about some situation when we choose to be emotional about it.

This is contrary to the most important myth about emotions, which is the situations myth. According to it, situations cause our emotions; we don't choose them.

Again, ordinary language reflects this common way of talking and thinking about emotions. "That's disgusting!" "What he did made me so angry!" "Weren't you surprised by our team's winning the championship?"

No. Situations never cause emotions. That's never the case because all (nonsubjective) situations are emotionally neutral. Suppose that your long-term lover died. Guess what? Death is as natural as birth. Births and deaths are facts of Becoming. That's all.

In order to understand them better, let's analyze emotions into their parts. Actually, situations are the *first* of their three parts.

A "situation" is just a state of affairs or event such as your lover's death that you take to be relevant to you. It's a fact. Of course, there are lots of situations that we don't take to be relevant to our lives with the result that we are never emotional about them. Suppose, for example, that it's snowing right now in Moscow. How do you feel about that? Unless you are in Moscow or have some other reason to care, you won't have any emotion at all about that situation.

Sometimes, of course, we misapprehend what is. If you think that your lover died and it turns out that your belief that your lover died is mistaken, you won't be emotional about your lover's death because it's a nonentity. It never happened. There's no reason to be upset. Once you realize the mistaken belief, your grief will soon dissipate. Very quickly the survival mechanism of the freeze, fight, or flight response that's caused by a cascade of hormones will diminish in intensity.

The *second* part of the analysis of emotions is that every emotion requires an egocentric evaluation about the situation at hand. This is **the essence of all emotions**. A positive evaluation has the form, "This is good for me." A negative evaluation has the form, "This is bad for me." If you are grief-stricken about your lover's death, supposing that that is the actual situation, it's not because your lover died; instead, it's because you decided that that situation was bad for you.

Although such decisions are typically instantaneous rather than deliberative, it is possible to slow them down sufficiently to understand that, nevertheless, they are decisions. It's important to realize this. Why? Ask yourself, 'Who makes my decisions?' Nobody except you could make them. Could you let someone else make all your decisions? Yes, at least theoretically you could do that. However, letting someone else decide for you would itself be a decision or, actually, a series of decisions. This explains why it's impossible for someone else to live your life. At least as an adult, your decisions are your responsibility and never someone else's responsibility.

The *third* part of the analysis of emotions is the accompanying physiological response and behavior. If your beloved dies, you learn of that death, and then you cry, your crying would be part of the third part of the analysis. It may be mild or intense depending upon the relative importance to you of the original situation. Similarly, your blood pressure or heart rate may increase.

Here's an important challenge for you: recall some specific, intense emotions from your past. Subject them to the analysis just given. If they fit, at least tentatively accept this analysis. If not, don't, and find a better one.

Perhaps this brief discussion of emotions has already dispelled significant confusion about them. Still, you wonder about the answer to the most important question about emotions, namely, **how can I flourish emotionally?** After all, if you are able to live better emotionally from now on, you'll automatically be demonstrating to others how to do the same. If so, you'll also automatically be reducing emotional suffering for yourself and others.

DENNIS E. BRADFORD, PH.D.

The natural and most important mistake with respect to living well emotionally is that people assume that it means attracting and attaching to positive emotions and avoiding or detaching quickly from negative emotions. The effort is to gain what we like and either to avoid or quickly dissolve what we don't like.

The theme that living well is all about gaining what we like and avoiding or eliminating what we don't like is called *"the way of the world."* It's called that because that's implicitly how most people live. They try to gain what they value and avoid or eliminate what they don't value. Isn't that so?

Whether or not it's the case that most people live that way doesn't really matter. What matters is if the wise live that way. We are not without role models. For example, do sages go through life trying to acquire more money or fame or lovers or status? Do they go through life worrying about their retirement plans, stock portfolios, or tax write-offs? Of course not. Many even take vows of poverty and celibacy. **Success is not a priority.** Often, it's a hindrance.

Mastery is our most important priority. Wisdom matters. Following the way of the world is a grave mistake for those who aspire to living well. The Buddha said explicitly, "Don't follow the way of the world" [from <u>The Dhammapada</u>].

Why did he say that? Because following the way of the world doesn't work for wisdom.

Again, with respect just to emotional wisdom, following the way of the world means trying to attract and attach to positive emotions while trying to avoid or detach from negative emotions. What's wrong with that?

What's wrong with following the way of the world in general is simple: whatever can be gained can also be lost and, whether you want them or not, life will provide you with situations you don't like and that you are powerless to change. Wisdom begins by apprehending and accepting reality.

Relate this to the first part of the analysis of emotions. Are you able to control life to the extent that it will never provide you with situations you may not like? Of course not. In terms of Becoming, your reality is the same as for all humans. Unless you happen to die young, you are going to grow old, become ill, and die – and there's nothing you can do about that.

Instead of fixating on the first part of the analysis of emotions, think hard about the second part. Again, it's not situations that cause emotional distress; it's our negative egocentric evaluations about situations that cause it. If so, obviously then, to delete the distress, delete the beliefs that cause it.

The key is that the evaluations are egocentric. Is there really a self, an ego/I, that is the continuant substratum underlying all experiences? Do you find it when you introspect? The Buddha didn't. Hume didn't. I don't. Maybe that's the problem.

In other words, **challenge the belief that's supporting the emotion**.

It's easy to do this conceptually. Why? It's impossible to evaluate a situation without at least taking its consequences into account. Even if it's not only the consequences that matter when we evaluate a situation, it would be absurd to say that they are not relevant. The problem is that all consequences of present situations occur in the future. Not only do we lack knowledge (demonstrative evidence) about the future, we also lack nondemonstrative evidence about the future! Why? It doesn't exist. There's nothing for such evidence to be about. The future is never anything more than some set of imagined thoughts.

Lacking any rational alternative, what we usually do is to assume that past and present connections will abide into the future. Often, they do. However, they may not – and, as Hume argued, there's no logical reason or necessity why they should. Your wife's being faithful to you yesterday does not entail that she will be faithful to you tomorrow.

So, to return to the example, suppose that your beloved wife of, say, twenty years was unexpectedly killed in an accident and you are now very sad. Why? You believe that her death was very bad for you.

Was it? Could it turn out in the long run to be very good for you? Perhaps, for example, you were so sad that you seriously committed to adopting a spiritual practice as a last alternative before suicide and eventually not only had an initial awakening experience but also infused that awakening throughout your life. Suppose, in other words, that you became a sage. Sages are the greatest lovers, friends to all, notoriously compassionate. Because there may be no psychological stress or any kind of psychological suffering after awakening experiences become fully integrated, your life may infinitely better than it ever was before your wife's death. If you were more attached to her than to anything else when she disappeared, in the short run that may have been the worst experience of your life; however, in the long run, it could have been the turning point that enabled you to live as well as it's possible to live. After all, **awakening is the greatest human experience.** In other words, your judgment that her death was very bad for you turned out in the long run to be a critical turn for the better in the sense that, despite the temporary suffering it caused, its beneficial consequences eventually far outweighed its negative consequences.

Hasn't that happened to you? I've certainly had similar experiences happen. Sometimes what I thought at the time was very bad for me turned out to be very good for me. Sometimes what I thought at the time was very good for me turned out to be very bad for me.

Evaluative judgments are always dubitable. Of course they are. There's no foreknowledge. As creatures in Becoming, we always have to wait for whatever unfolds.

Weakening the egocentric judgments at their centers weakens the emotions. Dissolving the egocentric judgments at their centers dissolves the emotions.

Attachment to thoughts separates. Detachment from thoughts unifies.

If you are suffering because of your wife's death, it's because you understand the situation to involve permanent separation and find that sad. Ultimately, it's attachment to your ego that is affecting your thinking.

Why not, then, detach from your ego? Diminish its power. How? Master some effective spiritual practice [as explained in the previous section].

However, you may object, won't that dissolve positive as well as negative emotions?

Yes, it will. That question itself, though, is just more clinging to the way of the world.

Do you think sages perpetually ride the emotional roller coaster up and down, alternating between emotions they like and ones they dislike? No. Instead, they get off the emotional roller coaster. If you seriously value living well, if you seriously value serenity, tranquility, and peace of mind, you will, too.

Does that mean that sages become dead like zombies going around without emotions?

Well, have you noticed any unhappy sages? While it's true, for example, that those who are fully awake may no longer experience the joy that alternates with sorrow, what replaces it is *abiding* joy or beatitude. Again, when they occasionally experience unwanted emotions, they are able to "cook" them quickly using the spiritual practice they have mastered to regain freedom from emotional bondage.

Sages are the happiest of all people. Most seem so radiant and overflowing with goodness that either they are constantly smiling or perpetually seem ready to break into a smile. Yes, there have been studies by social scientists of the degree of happiness reported by people that support this. This is why it's important not to interpret, say, the occasional notorious ferocity of a Zen master wielding a <u>kotsu</u> (baton, stick) to stimulate his or her disciples to practice more intensely as expressing anger; actually, although it may seem the opposite, it's an express of love or compassion. The roar of a lion does not necessarily mean that the lion is unhappy.

An excellent way to contrast a normal self and an awakened self is to consider their primordial emotional states. I argue in <u>Mastery in 7 Steps</u> that normal selves, selves bound to live only in Becoming, are naturally lazy, greedy, ambitious, impatient, selfish, vain, and ignorant [Chapter 2.5.]. As a consequence, since it thrives when people are greedy, ambitious, and selfish, it's not difficult to understand why capitalism works as well as it does [See below "Introduction to Living Well Financially."]. Capitalism is economic warfare in which individuals struggle to out-compete others. Put that way, isn't it obvious why **fear** is so prevalent in the lives of those who only live in Becoming? Anytime something is gained, there's fear that it can be lost. There's perpetual fear that, even if one is successful, eventually one will become unsuccessful. Fear is the breeding ground for other rampant emotions like anger and hatred. Whenever I encounter someone whose primary emotional orientation is fear, I take it that I'm encountering someone who lives only in Becoming.

What's the primary emotional orientation of a sage, of someone who is open to Being and not bound to life in Becoming? **Trust**. Fear and trust are opposites. Whenever I encounter someone whose primary emotional orientation is trust, I take it that I'm encountering someone who is open to Being. The more someone's life is pervaded by Being, the less lazy, greedy, ambitious, impatient, selfish, vain, and ignorant that person tends to be.

Which feels better, being fearful or being trusting? The answer is indubitable.

Why not find out for yourself how good it is to free yourself from emotional bondage by mastering some spiritual practice or other? Even regular practicing short of any awakening experience will make a significant difference in the quality of your emotional life. [I can assure you of that from my own experience.]

In other words, assuming that you are already doing what is required for living well spiritually [see the previous section], there's nothing else you need to be doing to live well emotionally. Even if you never become a sage, your future will be characterized by diminished emotional suffering and increased emotional freedom.

SUGGESTIONS FOR FURTHER READING

Bradford, D. Emotional Facelift
Bradford, D. How to Survive College Emotionally
Ekman, P. Emotions Revealed
Goleman, D. Emotional Intelligence

TIPS: Prolonged emotional distress is optional. If you would like a free, downloadable report I wrote on 3 harmful myths about emotions that keep many people stuck, go to: https://endfearfast.com/

If you are struggling with some powerful emotion like fear, anger, sadness, or grief, you may also still be able to schedule a no-cost, no-obligation one-on-one telephone session with me. Please read the report first. Then you may schedule the call at: https://calendly.com/dennis-47/session

If you know any adults who are hurting emotionally, consider passing these two tips along.

❖

Introduction to Living Well Morally

Recall that I'm here using 'morally' ('ethically') to refer to the chief subject matter of morality, namely, interpersonal relationships.

Everyone understands that the best relationships are loving ones. Let's start by admitting an obvious fact, namely, **loving relationships are difficult for everyone to create and sustain.**

As Jean-Paul Sartre famously wrote, "Hell is other people." Bertrand Russell once wrote something to the effect that loving humanity is easy, but loving individual humans is hard. Improving relationships is one of the three top topics that internet marketing gurus suggest to their students because it is both evergreen and popular. (The other two are making money and health, particularly fat loss.) It's evergreen or of perpetual interest because everyone struggles with relationships.

Friendship is the paradigm of a loving interpersonal relationship. Perhaps the most popular ideal of a loving relationship would be a lasting sexual relationship grounded upon a great friendship. Why? Although infrequent, such relationships are the most likely to be emotionally, sexually, and intellectually satisfying.

The most famous book of ethics in the western tradition is Aristotle's Nichomachean Ethics. ('Nicomachean' just refers to the name of its editor.) His main teaching in it on loving relationships is that it's best to think that **"your friend . . . is another yourself."** Notice [from the above section "Introduction to Living Well Spiritually"] that, the more you get out of your thoughts and into life, the easier it is to identify with the essence (Being) of others since it's the same as your essence.

Let's initially (A) review some of Aristotle's most important ideas about love, (B) evaluate them briefly, and (C) make them easier to actualize concretely.

A

The paradigm of a loving relationship is a "complete" friendship. What's that?

Complete friendships are contrasted with common "utility" friendships. Most friendships are utility friendships in which the participants befriend each other because they take the other person in the encounter to be useful. If it's restricted to the gym, a friendship with a strength training partner would be an example of a utility friendship. Another example would be if you regularly purchase a service or a product (for example, organic produce from a nearby farmer) from someone who gives you a special deal in return. Utility friendships are conditional and egocentric. Ordinary sex affairs or pleasure friendships are just varieties of utility friendships. There's nothing necessarily wrong with utility friendships. They can be mutually beneficial. Obviously, though, they are not loving relationships; instead, they are business arrangements.

By way of contrast, complete friendships are loving relationships in which the friends promote each other's good. It's not that they are using each other or simply enjoy sharing activities; it's that, ideally, each works hard, regularly, and selflessly to promote what is best for the other (instead of egocentrically using the other to promote what is best for himself or herself). Love is giving; it's false that it's taking. This is why only morally good people like sages (successful philosophers) are able to engage in complete friendships. It's only morally good people who are able to benefit others selflessly. Complete friends incessantly encourage and challenge each other to live better. This won't work unless they are both roughly equal in moral value and seriously want to live better.

Complete friendships take a lot of time and honest communication to create, but they are relatively long-lasting, especially when, as they should, the friends live together. This means that, at best, even a morally excellent person who is lucky will enjoy only a very small number of complete friendships in a lifetime. It's certainly possible for a morally good person never to enjoy one or never to enjoy more than one at a time.

They are aware of what their loving activity is creating. **To love is really to act frequently in such as way as to promote what is best for the beloved.** This requires honest communication; otherwise, how would one friend know what's best for the other?

Why bother to create a complete friendship? It's because morally good people enjoy acting excellently to benefit other morally good people. "[L]oving is like a production." A complete friendship is, in fact, a "reciprocated goodwill," a "mutual loving."

Like the Buddha, Aristotle realizes that the wise do not need friendships. They have a self-sufficiency that most people lack [as pointed out above]. Do not, then, assume that the wise ever attempt to establish complete friendships because they need them. Since sages are self-sufficient and do not need people to benefit them, they never seek complete friendships out of any sense of need. Instead, it's as if they were so overflowing with goodness that they want to share it: "the excellent person will need people for him to benefit."

B

There's a lot of practical wisdom in Aristotle's ideas about complete friendship, but they are theoretically inadequate for three reasons.

First, they are grounded upon a substance ontology rather than a nonsubstance ontology. Since [as I argued above] substance ontologies are unintelligible, the conceptual foundation for his ideas about friendship is unsatisfactory.

Second, they are grounded on the idea that persons have different moral values. That may be so, but [as I argued above] I accept the view that all human beings are of equal moral worth. Because we share the same essence (namely, Being), a peasant or a slave has the same moral value as a sage.

Third, Aristotle also makes the ignorant assumption that women cannot be sages. Women can not only be philosophers but successful philosophers. (In fact, although this may spring from specific cultural roles, it may well be that it's actually usually faster for women to enjoy awakening experiences than for men.)

However, even if this is correct, despite their theoretical inadequacy Aristotle's ideas about friendship are not only important but valuable. (Furthermore, even thinking through for ourselves why they are inadequate in theory can benefit us by increasing our understanding. One should study the history of philosophy to improve one's understanding rather than to find views worthy of attachment. Once one thinks through a view and tentatively adopts it, it becomes one's own, but one should always remain open-minded and willing to reconsider it. Always be ready to stop being blinded by views by always being willing to detach from them. [Marx gives an example of how this works in the "Introduction to Flourishing Financially" section below.]) Why?

It's his emphasis on encouraging and challenging each other to live better. Here's how this works.

We've seen that to be a philosopher is to be a lover of wisdom or living well. Unlike nonphilosophers who content themselves with settle-for lives, philosophers are serious about living better. A sage is a philosopher who has succeeded in living wisely or well. They are people who have awakened, opened to Being, and integrated that awakening throughout their lives.

What's the best group of people with whom to create a friendship? Sages, of course. They, though, are few and far between.

What's the second-best group of people with whom to create a friendship? Philosophers, genuine seekers who are still seriously trying to live better. Although also uncommon, they are much more common than successful seekers.

What's the worst group of people with whom to create a friendship? Nonphilosophers who are not even trying to live better. If you want a good exercise in frustration, try helping someone to live better who isn't interested in living better! Nonphilosophers killed Socrates for doing that.

In other words, if we transform Aristotle's thinking about people having different moral values into thinking about the life goals that people actually have, we have a way to rank them without having to accept any notion that some people are of greater moral worth than other people.

If your friend is a philosopher, whether successful or not yet living well, your friend will be receptive to your encouraging or challenging him or her in terms of living better. Also, the less egocentric or more awake your friend is, the better your friend will be at encouraging or challenging you to live better.

One takeaway here is to try to make complete friendships only with other philosophers, which is a charitable interpretation of part of what Aristotle is claiming.

Nietzsche warns us never to be second in love. Let's develop this idea.

Suppose that you and S[omeone] are in the process of creating a complete friendship. Why not make that process fun by making it into a kind of game?

After all, if you are letting S out-love you, you are losing your encounter with S. Why not skillfully encourage S to live better? Why not develop your understanding, your compassion, and your interpersonal skills to become a better lover? Why not *challenge yourself daily* to do better every day by increasing your understanding, compassion, and interpersonal skills to become a better lover? Why not daily practice to reduce your egocentricity? Why not then regularly use those enhanced abilities to encourage S skillfully (as well as yourself) to live better?

WARNING: this only works if S is a philosopher. Otherwise, you'll likely just fail at what you are trying to do and succeed only in stimulating resentment. It's like trying to teach a pig to sing. Furthermore, as the Buddha emphasized, this must be done skillfully. In other words, you not only need to understand what would be best for S but also you need to have practical wisdom to encourage S successfully. How?

C

Start by becoming a skillful listener. Challenge yourself to learn to listen deeply. Perhaps the greatest gift you can give another person is your full attention. There are a number of helpful books available on how to listen deeply and nonjudgmentally. Paying attention isn't easy because healthy brains constantly generate thoughts about the past and about the future. The purpose of a spiritual practice is not necessarily to stop thoughts from arising automatically; instead, it's to stop automatically attaching to them when they do arise. Would you like to become a better lover? Then practice daily paying full attention to the present moment. [How? As explained above, any classical practice such as Aliveness Awareness or zazen may be used.] When your friend is in front of you, pay full attention to what your friend is trying to communicate.

In *Stress Reduction Wizardry* I explained that different people have different learning styles. Although it's natural, it's a mistake to assume that everyone else has the same learning style that you have. Find out your friend's primary learning style and use that information.

In <u>The Five Love Languages</u>, Gary Chapman argues that there's a similar situation with love languages. Different people have different love languages. Although it's natural, it's a mistake to assume that everyone else has the same love language that you have.

Therefore, if you want to communicate with S effectively and efficiently, you should communicate your love for S in S's love language whether or not S's love language happens to be the same as yours. This is especially important in erotic relationships. Even when two people genuinely love each other, they may not communicate well. If failing to communicate well isn't the number one cause of break-ups, it's certainly among the most important.

So, it's critical to ensure that you understand S's primary language.

When it comes to learning styles, although there are four different ones, each individual may be a unique blend of the four. When teaching someone, focus on that person's primary learning style.

When it comes to love languages, although there are five different ones, each individual may prefer a unique blend of the five. When loving someone, focus on that person's primary love language.

When it comes to love's beginning, Chapman correctly dismisses the euphoric experience of falling in love, which isn't love at all. Furthermore, unlike a normal complete friendship, it's very impermanent.

Genuine love comes from Being [see the section "Introduction to Living Well Spiritually" above]. In fact, it's not wholly misleading simply to identify love and Being (for example, "God is love").

One way to understand that is to understand that opening to Being requires no-thought. The ego is a creature of thought. **No thought, no ego**. Genuine love requires understanding what is best for the beloved and repeatedly attempting to give or stimulate it. It's not getting something you might enjoy; instead, it's frequently doing something for your beloved with no thought of getting anything in return, which is why it's unconditional. Forget what you want and promote S's well-being. This explains why sages are the greatest lovers. They are the least egocentric of all people. (Yes, sages still have egos, but the egoic structure of a fully awakened sage is very different from the structures of the egos the rest of us have.)

The more awake you are, the easier it will be for you to get outside yourself. If you are normally egocentric, you'll just assume that S also speaks your love language. If you are less than normally egocentric, you may, at least after reading this, pause and try to figure out what S's love language is so that you are able to communicate better with S.

TIP: Why not ask?

Words of affirmation are one love language. Build up S's confidence with verbal compliments when S does well and words of appreciation for the way S is. Instead of abusing or criticizing S, instead of complaining about S or what S has done or failed to do, use language that is unfailingly kind. Always let your language be soft, gentle and inspiring. It's true that nobody else, including and especially you, can live well for S. However, if S's love language is words of affirmation, there may be nothing better you can do to love S and encourage or even inspire S to live better than to use affirmative language. For example, never demand, only request.

Quality time is a second love language. Simple. Spend time giving S your undivided attention. If you talk when you are together, let the conversation be a sympathetic dialogue. Practice deep, nonjudgmental listening when S talks. Don't interrupt, either. Ask questions with a genuine desire to understand. If there's no need to talk when you are together, enjoy and extend the comfortable silence of complete friendship.

Giving gifts is a third love language. Giving gifts is a classic way of expressing love. A "gift" here is something physical. S can hold it and think 'my friend was thinking of me.' It doesn't have to be anything expensive; it doesn't need to cost any money at all. It only needs to be thoughtful. What's the spirit of love? Giving (as opposed to taking).

Acts of service is a fourth love language. This is expressing love for S by giving something that S values to S. Do something for S. For example, wash S's car or go to a library and borrow a book to loan to S because you know that S will enjoy it. Of course, give acts of service freely and without expecting anything in return.

Physical touches are a fifth love language. If S is your lover, he or she may deeply appreciate physical expressions of love. It doesn't have to be sexual intercourse. It can be simply touching S on the shoulder as you pass by or giving S a kiss. Holding hands when you are sitting or walking together can decrease the feeling of separation. Even if S isn't your lover, there are occasions when, for example, a hearty hug is just perfect for the moment.

Assuming that you are trying to establish a loving relationship with S, what is S's primary love language? What is S's secondary love language? Find out and then use that information.

Emergencies or times of crisis are wonderful opportunities for expressing love.

Is S loving you more than you are loving S? If so, get busy. You are losing the game.

There's no downside to becoming a better lover.

The real key to becoming a better lover is ego reduction. If, as I hope, you are spending an hour or two daily engaged with an effective spiritual practice and deliberately trying to infuse the deep stillness it engenders throughout the rest of your life, you are already doing what is essential for living well morally.

In other words, the moral imperative is the same as the spiritual imperative: **Wake up!**

Reality is the obstructed obvious. What's obstructing reality? Thoughts [judgments, conceptualizations]. Drop them and you may be amazed at how easy it becomes to identify with others.

Identifying with others is the key to compassion and love. Wake up to live and love better. You may just discover for yourself that Being is the source of all love. When we live in reality, love is easier and much more natural than it is when we live in unreality, our own private surrealities.

The fact that loving relationships are difficult for everyone to create and sustain may be a blessing in disguise. They are great opportunities for practicing and they are so obviously valuable that recognition of that fact provides motivation for practicing. In other words, from the standpoint of having a peaceful mind, it's easier to live in solitude than it is even to live with someone with whom one has created a complete friendship. However, one of the disadvantages of living in solitude is that the daily interaction with another that often causes common challenges is absent. The best way to dissolve those challenges is to achieve union in Being and the best way to do that is to master a spiritual practice together.

SUGGESTIONS FOR FURTHER READING

Aristotle. Nicomachean Ethics. T. Irwin, tr., or J. Sachs, tr.
Blanton, B. Radical Honesty
Bradford, D. Love and Respect
Brown, M. Stone Soup
Cicero, "Laelius: On Friendship," in On the Good Life
Fisher, B. Rebuilding
Giblin, L. Skill With People
Hanh, Thich Nhat. Teachings on Love

Introduction to Living Well Intellectually

The belief that literacy is required for living well is false. Surprised?

It's true that some good thinking is required for living well. The only exceptions would be those probably extremely infrequent cases of being naturally awake and those cases in which great suffering stimulates the shift from a normal to an awakened self. Even when stimulated by a crisis, however, it can be extremely beneficial to encounter someone, whether through the spoken or written word, to explain what has happened. (Even a relatively short explanation such as the section above on living well spiritually may be all that's required.)

The most efficient way to encounter good thinking is by reading. Why? We are often able to read at least five times faster than we are able to talk. So listening to someone talk or watching a video in which someone talks (such as *Stress Reduction Wizardry*) requires much more time than would be required simply to read the words.

On the other hand, many people don't read words as if their author were speaking to them. They find reading less engaging that being spoken to. Many enjoy watching, say, a video more than reading an essay or even a story.

Since you are reading this, you are already literate. You've already paid the price of having that skill. If you do not read, you have no advantage over someone who cannot read.

I've always believed that it's possible to get as good an education in a well-stocked public library as it is going to college. On the other hand, it's a lot easier, safer, and more efficient doing it with the guidance of good teachers by going through the normal procedure of graduating with a liberal arts major as an undergraduate and then proceeding on to some appropriate graduate degree. Why not learn from the successes and failures of others? The only alternative is inevitably slower and creates more dissatisfactions.

Why a liberal arts degree? My view is that the purpose of an undergraduate education is to spawn an identity crisis in a safe, productive environment. Undergraduates should ask the existential questions. *Who am I? What is my true nature? How did I get here? What am I supposed to be doing with my life? What is living well like?* Coming up with coherent, at least tentative answers to such questions should precede any kind of job or career training. Why even assume that a student should be preparing for a job or a career? Although it's especially true with respect to philosophy, liberal arts majors are more likely to develop well-conceived answers to the important questions than, say, business, science, or mathematics majors. Focusing on human nature and maximizing its potential should precede decisions directly related to money making.

Yes, formal education is expensive. Especially if it's not just job training, it may not even pay off financially in the long run. However, if you happened to have the opportunity of attending a good college and perhaps even going on to graduate school and took advantage of it, good for you! If not, if doing that wasn't a viable option for whatever reason, that's alright. If literacy isn't required for sagehood, neither is a bachelor's nor an advanced degree.

Given that you are literate and already able to open your mind to stimulation by good teachers and writers, I've included in each of these sections some books that I recommend for your continuing education. None are very expensive and, if you are able to borrow them from a library, accessing their contents will only cost you some time, which I hope and believe you'll find to be time well spent. [If you have feedback on any of them you'd like to share with me, I'd appreciate receiving it.]

What, really, is it to live well? I suggest that you approach reading as trying to come to a clear understanding of your place in the world, in other words, where your consciousness actually exists right now in relation to the unimaginably large universe as a whole and the incredibly small world of quantum physics. My own ideas about that are insufficiently well-formed to share, but, if you read some of the books that I recommend here such as those by E. Tolle and S. Taylor (as well as, of course, related works by other authors such as Hegel) by considering seriously the possibility that Becoming may be produced by Being, your thinking may be stretched in a new direction.

Assuming that you are not already a sage, if you haven't already established the practice, I recommend reading for at least **20 or 30 minutes daily**.

It's true that I've not personally met many sages, but I encountered quite a few in various other ways and almost without exception these days they not only read but write. Why writing? Don't think of it as merely being a way of recording thinking; instead, think of it as a way of thinking. Anyone who is able to write clearly is someone who is able to think clearly. Should thinking be clear or muddled? Going through life as confused as most adults seem to be is a predisposition to a life of unnecessary dissatisfaction.

It's not infrequently remarked that it makes little sense to try to reinvent the wheel. **Genuine creativity comes after opening to Being**. Until you have opened to Being yourself, follow others who have succeeded and mastered life. Then write or do whatever suits your talents and interests.

Though admiring his work, my mother never really liked Joseph Conrad's written stories. On the other hand, I always liked them from the first one I read. Of course, I, too, admired them, partly because of the fact that English, the language he wrote in and mastered, was not his primary language. I think I especially liked them, though, because of the fact that he really lived a lot more life than most authors before even starting to write.

A lot of people have tried to master life as well as succeed in various aspects of it. The only important thesis in this section is that, *if you don't read regularly, you are being foolish*. Learning from the successes and mistakes of others is, almost without exception, easier and faster than learning from your own. Why not be as successful and masterful as possible?

Books, perhaps even this one, may shorten your learning curve. Stay curious about living well and read every day to benefit from enabling others to share their judgments and experiences with you. Remember, you are not just doing this for egocentric reasons. The better you live, the more you'll automatically be demonstrating to others how to live. Keep that in mind whenever you feel disinclined to read.

The danger in our age of incessant distractions is not attachment to book learning. The danger is insufficiently tapping into the wisdom of authors. There's no reason to let that happen to you. Unless you are already a sage or on a spiritual retreat, please **make reading well daily a habit**. By 'reading well' I mean reading edifying material and paying full and critical attention to it.

A final tip: realize that *information consumes attention*. The more you pay attention to information gleaned from most content sources such as telephones, television, movies, and the world wide web, the more your attention is consumed. We all only ever get so much attention.

Of course, there's nothing necessarily wrong with, say, watching a talk by a sage on YouTube or enjoying an occasional movie or chat with a friend. They can be helpful and enjoyable. There's nothing necessarily wrong with reading pulp fiction either. My experience has been that someone who regularly reads anything is more likely to become a better friend than a nonreader.

Be careful, though, to limit the information you consume lest it consume too much of your attention. For example, especially if the alternative is a temptation, put yourself on a news fast. It's easy for many people to become news junkies. If you discover that tendency in yourself, by all means read a good weekly news magazine like *The Economist* to keep informed, but limit severely or stop radio and television news programs – and never consume them in the morning or afternoon when you are likely to be at your most creative. Besides, if you have never seriously studied political philosophy, you've never even established a good framework for understanding historical or current events.

Instead of paying attention to what others are doing or failing to do, work on yourself. The world would be a better place if, as the Buddha said, people refrained from going around bothering others.

SUGGESTIONS FOR FURTHER READING

Bradford, D. The Meditative Approach to Philosophy
Cohen, A. Are You As Happy As Your Dog?
Gallway, W. T. The Inner Game of Tennis
Harari, Y.N. Homo Deus
Harari, Y.N. Sapiens
Hayes, S. C., and Smith, S. Get Out of Your Mind & Into Your Life
Hedges, B. Read & Grow Rich
Norrettranders. T. The User Illusion

---- ❖ ----

Introduction to Living Well Physically

Living well is impossible without living. It doesn't take that much more time and effort to tend your body well than to treat it poorly. The extra care is worth it.

On the other hand, flourishing physically is not the purpose of life. No matter how young, healthy, fit, and strong you are, your death is certain. What's uncertain is only its timing. The law is inexorable: all living organisms die. All that begins to exist also ceases to exist.

In general, much of what determines our physical well-being is beyond our control. We do not control our genetic endowment, which includes genetic diseases.

In specific, much of what determines our physical well-being is also beyond our control. For example, there's nothing you can do about it if you suffered in childhood from nutritional deficiencies or serious accidents that may have left you chronically ill, crippled, or deformed.

Wisdom begins with accepting reality. You don't have to like it to accept it. Since it already is, it's foolish and futile to fight it. Whatever your physical condition, accept it.

Then ask: 'Is there any way I might be able to improve it?' If not, skip to the next section.

If so, 'Would trying to improve it be worth it?' If not, skip to the next section.

WARNING: Always consult your personal physician or other licensed medical practitioner before changing your dietary or exercise habits. Take advice only after a thorough physical examination from someone who demonstrates excellent understanding of human dietary and exercise needs. Unfortunately, when it comes to preventive medicine, in my experience most western physicians lack a good understanding of either.

If you are still here, it's likely because you have an interest in improving your body composition. Your body is composed of fat (adipose tissue) and everything that isn't fat (primarily muscle and bone in addition to your other organs and central nervous system). Your lean-body mass is your biologically active tissue, namely, your muscles, bones, and vital organs.

Muscle mass declines with age and the rate of loss typically accelerates after the mid-40's. The way to retard this decline is with effective strength training and maintaining a relatively high level of anabolic hormones. Typically, not only do most people lose a high percentage of their muscle cells by age 70, but also the remaining cells start to atrophy. However, since strength training can retard this decline in muscle strength and size, it's not inevitable, at least until very old age.

Typically, too, our basal metabolic rate (BMR, caloric expenditure at rest) declines with age. However, it's the reduced muscle mass of elderly people that seems primarily responsible for this. If so, when effective strength training retards the typical reduction in muscle mass, it will also retard the BMR decline.

Two-thirds of Americans are either overweight or obese. That's not good in terms of physical health. Understanding that, many people obsess about being too fat. That's a mistake. Why? Being too fat is really only a consequence of the problem. Fixing it temporarily by using some reducing diet or other doesn't solve the problem. In fact, it typically makes it worse. Yes, you may want to carry less fat to be healthier and look better, but the right way to do that is to focus on solving the underlying problem.

First, forget about your body weight. It doesn't matter. Your body composition does matter when it comes to your health and appearance. It makes a big difference whether you are 15% body fat or 40% body fat. In general, adult women should have less than 20% body fat and adult men should have less than 15%. (Don't confuse percentage of body fat with BMI.)

Second, teach yourself the best current theory about eating well and exercising well and then apply what you've learned to your own case with an open mind. If you are interested in flourishing spiritually, it's important to realize that there is no one spiritual practice that is best for everyone. Similarly, if you are interested in flourishing physically, it's important to realize that there is no one dietary or exercise program that is best for everyone. What's best for you? Keep testing and making adjustments according to the feedback you receive.

Our bodies change from one moment to the next. So, don't be surprised that a program that worked well for you yesterday fails to work well today and needs to be revised in accordance with changing circumstances. This is a concrete example of what it means to live an examined life. Detachment is the key. Instead of fanatically attaching to some theoretical program that you think should work, examine whether or not it actually is working well. If so, continue. If not, revise it and test something else.

Third, instead of focusing on a consequence of being well physically, focus on what really matters. What really matters in terms of your physical health is your lung power, your aerobic capacity. This is usually measured in terms of your maximal oxygen intake (VO_2max). Many experts believe that **VO_2max is the single most important indicator of your health and predictor of your future health**. Typically, most people experience a decline in their aerobic capacity as they age. Furthermore, peak heart rate decreases with age. Nevertheless, older people who exercise properly can achieve VO$_2$max levels equivalent to those of younger people.

As our bodies age, our organs become less efficient. Our bodies take up blood sugar (glucose) and productively use it. Our ability to do this is called "glucose tolerance" and levels of blood sugar tend to increase with age. This increases the risk of Type II diabetes, which has now reached epidemic proportions. A higher percentage of body fat and physical inactivity are direct causes of creeping glucose intolerance.

Bones are living tissue. The older we become, the more likely our bones will experience a decline in their mineral content, which leaves us with weaker, more brittle skeletons. More trabecular bone than cortical bone mass is lost as we age (and the rate of bone loss is faster in women than in men). Fortunately, strength training and other weight-bearing exercise can retard this decline. Deliberately stressing a bone safely and repeatedly will cause it to strengthen. Furthermore, exercise may help improve the body's calcium absorption.

The body's critical thermoregulatory ability diminishes with age. The elderly have a lessened ability to shiver as well as a reduced sensation of thirst. It's not surprising, then, that many elderly people drink too little water. Furthermore, again, as we age our organs begin to work less efficiently. For example, the kidneys of 70-year-olds usually filter waste out of the blood half as fast as happened when they were 30. Along with reduced renal [kidney] function, the elderly have an impaired ability to concentrate urine. This helps to explain why the thermoregulatory ability diminishes with age. Maintaining a good or high level of cardiovascular fitness and forcing yourself to drink more water especially when you are older and not thirsty are ways of maintaining and repairing your body's thermoregulatory ability.

Heart disease is the number one killer in America. An important risk factor with respect to heart disease is your cholesterol/HDL ratio, which is simply your total cholesterol level divided by your HDL-cholesterol. Essentially, the lower your cholesterol/HDL ratio, the better. It's best to keep it at 4.5 or lower and, with proper diet and exercise, it's possible to do that indefinitely.

Hypertension (abnormally high blood pressure) is a condition that also need not increase with age. However, in America, it, too, has become an epidemic. Scientists understand that this doesn't need to happen for the simple reason that there are societies in which it doesn't happen.

There's a big takeaway from all this, namely, **your body's age is not necessarily its chronological age**.

If you would like to live a long, healthy life, there are regular actions, namely, eating well and exercising well, that you can take that will increase you chances of doing that.

While the way that I think of something is not necessarily the way you should think of it and certainly may not be the best way to think of it, here's the way I think of doing what is reasonable to do in terms of enjoying a long, healthy life: it's **80% eating well and 20% exercising well**.

BACKGROUND

Especially over the last century or two, lots of very clever scientists have done a lot of excellent work figuring out how we human beings came to be as we are. It's true that science never yields knowledge (demonstrative evidence), but the non-demonstrative evidence that has accumulated is very impressive. It's a fascinating story that has direct relevance to how we should both eat and exercise *if* our goal is to live as long and healthy lives as possible. If that's not what you value, skip to the next section.

Let's begin with **natural eating**. By 'natural' I'm of course thinking of what is natural for human beings.

Philosophers live examined lives. They are not only open-minded, but they are persistently curious and always ready to re-examine their own beliefs. At least within their fields of expertise, the best scientists, too, are like that.

When it comes to health and preventive medicine, I've recently become very impressed by the work of Steven Gundry, M.D. I've struggled for decades trying to figure out how to eat well for health and longevity. Gundry's work has finally answered some important questions I've had. Many of the ideas that follow here are heavily influenced by his writings. Here's my suggestion for you if you also find that what follows here makes a lot of sense: commit yourself seriously to doing what he recommends for just 30 days. This would be an important test. It's likely that you'll still be alive 31 days from now anyway. If you do, I predict that you'll not only feel better and be more energetic after following his recommendations for 30 days, but also you'll be healthier and probably a little lighter. If so, that will help provide you with the motivation to continue to eat as he recommends. The easiest way to do that is to read and follow the plan in his The Plant Paradox Quick and Easy.

Our beautiful planet is about 4.5 billion years old. Plants appeared about 450 million years ago. (Not interested in plants? If a statistic I encountered recently is correct, we share about 25% of our DNA with trees! If so, from a biological perspective we are much more like plants than we may initially think.) Insects followed about 110 million years later – and they started eating plants.

That caused a serious problem for plants. Just like us, plants want to survive, reproduce, and ensure the survival of their offspring. Think of the seeds of plants as their babies. It's as if plants didn't want their babies eaten by insects or, later, other kinds of animals; they had to do something.

They did. They produced **anti-nutrients** such as lectins, phytates, trypsin inhibitors, tannins, and alkaloids in an effort to cause both short-term and long-term distress to those who ate them. Of course, over time the plant-eaters evolved defenses against anti-nutrients and the biological struggle continues.

EATING WELL

According to Gundry, foods that are high in lectins, which are a kind of protein, are particularly damaging to us in four ways. They do massive digestive damage. By punching holes in the lining of our intestines, they increase our chances of having a leaky gut. By clogging insulin receptors, they increase appetite because we don't feel as full as we should after eating, which stimulates overeating and fat gain. They also weaken blood vessels, which increases the risk of cardiovascular disease.

If so, the question becomes: 'How can we protect ourselves from anti-nutrients like lectins?'

The answer is obvious: 'Stop eating foods that are high in anti-nutrients like lectins.' Unfortunately, in practice, that's not easy to do. Still, it's the right answer. Gundry argues that what we should adopt is "a microbiome- and mitochondria-contic program that recommends a diverse array of the right plant foods at the right time, prepared in the right way, in the right amounts" [from The Plant Paradox].

Think of your body as like a flexible tube with one end being the mouth and the other end being the anus. Surprisingly, the lining or wall of your gastrointestinal tract [gut] is just one cell thick; it's extremely thin. Its inside is lined with mucus, which is an additional protective barrier. The contents of your gut are actually external to your body just like the way that the air inside a tube or pipe is external to it even though it's inside it. Your gut wall functions to (i) keep certain "bad" food particles in it to be excreted later as waste and (ii) to permit other "good" food particles (such as digested food, minerals, amino acids, fatty acids, and sugars) to pass through it in order to enter the bloodstream and nourish you.

Your gut contents are a "microbiome" where millions of microbes live. Since they help digest food and help maintain our immune system, their health is of critical importance to our health. *If your microbiome is flourishing and the lining of your gut is intact, you are much more likely to be healthy than otherwise. If your microbiome is unhealthy or the lining of your gut has holes in it, you are much more likely to be unhealthy than otherwise.*

You've likely heard of the inflammation theory of disease. There's little doubt anymore that widespread inflammation is a key indicator of ill health. What, though, is the root cause of inflammation? Gundry argues that it's leaky gut. That occurs when your immune system attacks lipopolysaccharides that have escaped through your gut wall into your body and have then been identified by your immune system, which begins to fight them. A weakened microbiome not only causes us to gain fat, but it also seems to be linked to diabetes, heart disease, and dementia.

Human beings have been around for only about 200,000 or 250,000 years. Until the first agricultural revolution about 10,000 or 12,000 years ago after the end of the last Ice Age, they were all hunter-gatherers. They ate fewer lectin-rich plants than we do today (as well as, of course, eating many different kinds of plants and natural flesh foods). They also had to endure periods of food scarcity.

Eventually, some of our ancestors figured out how to cultivate grains and beans, which helped in times when other foods were scarce because they could not only be processed and eaten but they also could be stored for later use. This seemed like a great advance, but, as many modern researchers have demonstrated, it came at a serious cost to human health. We now understand why: grains and beans are lectin-rich foods. They are high in anti-nutrients.

The human microbiome has not had sufficient time to evolve the ability to handle these foods well.

Furthermore, a few centuries ago when Europeans discovered the new world, they also discovered new world crops such as corn, squash, tomatoes, peppers, quinoa, and others. While Native American populations had had up to 15,000 years of exposure to these plants and learned how to prepare them to minimize the harmful effects of the lectins they contain, that wasn't true for European, African, and Asian populations.

Furthermore, just since the 1950's processed foods, which are often made from grains and oils that are high in lectins, have become very popular, in part because they taste good and are relatively inexpensive. Many supposedly healthful foods such as tofu, whole grains, brown rice, low-fat dairy products, and vegetable oils actually harm our health.

Furthermore, instead of eating wild-caught game and fish like our hunter-gatherer ancestors, when we eat flesh-foods we often eat them from animals that have been farm-raised. In terms of health, it's one thing to eat, say, flesh from sockeye salmon or elk. It's another thing to eat fish from a fish farm or beef from a cattle ranch that have been fed high-lectin grains. Assuming that you eat flesh foods at all, before eating any, ask 'What did the food that I am eating eat?' If the animals that you eat have an unnatural diet, guess what? So do you.

This makes a lot of sense, doesn't it? It's has to a lot of people, which is a chief reason "neanderthin" or "paleo" diets have grown in popularity in the last quarter century. *In terms of health and longevity, it's simply a good idea to eat, and to exercise, a lot more like our hunter-gatherer ancestors. It's a more natural way.*

Instead of thinking back just 20,000 or 200,000 years to our homo sapiens ancestors, though, realize that they didn't suddenly appear from nothing. Why not go back to our proto-human ancestors of, say, 5,000,000 or 10,000,000 or 20,000,000 years ago? Do that to learn what they ate and you'll solidify the judgment that, for human beings, **eating plant foods should be the cornerstone of a healthy diet.**

Nor are we limited to eating plant foods. That's one of the many blessings of civilization. The next time you go to a grocery store, you'll likely be able to purchase such healthful foods as eggs from pastured chickens, wild-caught salmon, and grass-fed and finished bison or beef. If you are a vegan or a vegetarian, you won't, but the point is that you have that option.

You are going to eat anyway. Eating well need not take much more time than eating poorly. Yes, you may have to think ahead and avoid fast-food restaurants, but those are minor costs for major benefits.

The first rule of eating well and exercising well should be: *be kind to yourself.* In other words, don't make things worse. Reduce the anti-nutrients you consume. Either avoid plants that are high in them or at least prepare them in ways that minimize their negative impacts on your body. For example, if you are going to make a tomato sauce anyway, at least remove the skin and seeds from the tomato because that's where most of the lectins are.

We've failed to do that. The result is that we are living with epidemics of heart disease, obesity, Type II diabetes, hypertension, cancer and other diseases. Our ancestors prior to the first agricultural revolution simply didn't suffer from such health problems to the extent that we do. If we emulate them, if we are kind to our bodies, we can not only increase our odds of living longer and healthier but also we can simultaneously enjoy the blessings of civilization. It's better for other animals and the planet as well.

How? There are lots of recipes and meal plans available. [See some of the listings in SUGGESTIONS FOR FURTHER READING below.]

The most important rule for eating well for health and nutrition is to **avoid or at least minimize consumption of foods that are high in anti-nutrients.** These include refined, starchy foods such as bread, cereal, cookies, crackers, pasta, pastries, potatoes, and potato chips. They also include grains, pseudo-grains, and grasses such as barley; buckwheat; corn and anything made from corn such as cornstarch, corn syrup and tortillas; oats; rye; wheat and anything made from wheat; and wild rice. They also include sugar and sugar substitutes including granulated sugar (even organic cane sugar), diet drinks, maltodextrin, aspartame, sucralose, acesulfame K, and saccharin. Avoid many offending vegetables such as beans, bean sprouts, chickpeas, green beans, legumes, lentils, peas including sugar snap peas, soy and soy protein, textured vegetable protein, and tofu. Many nuts and seeds don't make the cut including almonds, cashews, peanuts, pumpkin seeds, and sunflower seeds. There are a few acceptable fruits and berries such as avocado permitted in moderation, but almost all fruits are particularly high in lectins so you should avoid bell peppers, chili peppers, cucumbers, eggplant, melons, tomatoes, and zucchini. Avoid all non-southern European cow's milk products such as butter, cheese, cottage cheese, frozen yogurt, ice cream, kefir, milk, ricotta cheese and yogurt including Greek yogurt because they contain casein A1. Avoid nearly all common oils such as canola, corn, cottonseed, grape seed, partially hydrogenated, peanut, safflower, soy, and vegetable as well as many common seasonings such as ketchup, mayonnaise, soy sauce, and steak sauces.

Wow! You may be wondering 'What's left?'

Actually, there's a lot left and I encourage you to consult Gundry's writings for lists of acceptable foods. There are, for example, plenty of different kinds of vegetables, including cruciferous vegetables, left; leafy greens; avocadoes (up to one daily); olives; many kinds of oils including avocado oil, extra virgin olive oil, perilla oil, and walnut oil; many kinds of nuts and seeds in limited quantities including Brazil nuts, chestnuts, co-conuts (including unsweetened coconut milk dairy substitute), flax seeds, hazelnuts, macadamia nuts, pecans, pistachios, pine nuts, tahini, and walnuts; multiple kinds of resistant starches and acceptable noodles; wild-caught fish (up to 4 oz. daily); pastured poultry; grass fed and finished meats (up to 4 oz. daily); occasional small servings of some in-season fruits; some dairy products and dairy product replacements including various kinds of cheeses, butters, yogurts, and milks; some energy bars (up to 1 daily); multiple kinds of herbs, seasonings, and condiments; multiple kinds of flours; many kinds of sweeteners; and even many kinds of chocolate and frozen desserts. In short, you are not going to starve. Your ancestors didn't!

Let me give you a sample of one of my actual daily meal plans (even though, as usual in this and other areas, I don't even pretend to be an excellent role model).

Before every meal, please remind yourself of why you are eating. If, for example, it's to sustain your life in order to lead an awakened life, say or think that. Please be grateful; give thanks to all the beings who contributed to your meal. Resolve to eat moderately and unlike a glutton.

Meals do not have to be complex. Being lazy, I usually prefer to keep them simple. It's easy, if you prefer, to spend a lot of time preparing meals.

BREAKFAST

I've tweaked what I consume for breakfast many times over the years. I'm pleased with what I use now. It consists of 2 drinks. The second is a modified version of a recipe from Gundry's The Plant Paradox Cookbook.

1. Thoroughly mix 1 heaping T psyllium whole husks in 1 cup of warm water. It's a good idea also to add a serving of powdered greens (such as Primal Plants from GundryMD) as well as something such as Bio Complete 3

from GundryMD for probiotics, prebiotics, and postbiotics. (To get the warm water, instead of using it from a hot water tap, start with cold water and heat it.) Drink immediately.

2. Ingredients

1 cup (8 fluid ounces) freshly brewed coffee

1 cup (8 fluid ounces) organic, unsweetened coconut milk

¼ t cinnamon

1 packet organic stevia

1 scoop Heart Defense from GundryMD or 2 T unsweetened natural cocoa powder

2 T extra-virgin olive oil [I use expensive, polyphenol-rich oil from GundryMD]

1 t Benefiber

2 ice cubes (optional)

Procedure Put the coconut milk, cinnamon, stevia, Benefiber, and Heart Defense into a blender. Pulse it on high speed a couple of times to blend. Add the coffee and olive oil. Pulse to blend thoroughly. If you prefer them, add the ice cubes. Cover blender and pulse until the ice cubes dissolve. Drink immediately.

MID-MORNING

1 hot cup of organic mint tea w 1 packet organic stevia

1/4 cup walnuts

LUNCH

½ to 1 cup organic broccoli with homemade oil & vinegar dressing

2 cooked eggs from pastured chickens, scrambled

2 slices of prosciutto, heated

[To make the dressing, blend extra-virgin olive oil with organic balsamic vinegar 50/50 or 60/40. Optional: add 1 T Dijon mustard.]

AFTERNOON [post-nap!]
1 hot cup of green tea w 1 packet of organic stevia

DINNER
[If you don't drink alcohol, don't start. If you are, like me, a drinker, it's fine to have 1 drink daily for a woman or 1 or 2 drinks daily for a man. A drink is either 5 ounces of (preferably red) wine or 1 shot of gin or dark spirits if you follow Gundry's advice.]

1 drink made with a glass of mineral water, 2 T balsamic vinegar, 1 scoop of Vital Reds from GundryMD (optional), and 1 or 2 shots of gin (optional)

1 large green organic salad (with lots of organic spinach) with homemade oil & vinegar dressing [recipe above]

1 Hass avocado

4 ounces of sockeye salmon fillet or grilled venison burger or grass fed and finished beefsteak

2 small pieces of dark chocolate (70% cacao or greater)

EVENING SNACK
¼ c pistachio nuts or macadamia nuts

some (black and/or green) olives

I also take some daily supplements such as folic acid, vitamin c, vitamin D_3, potassium, a multivitamin/multimineral, and krill or fish oil. [For Gundry's advice on supplements, see Chapter 11 of The Longevity Paradox.]

If you are not now eating well for health and longevity and eat as Gundry recommends as a test for just four weeks, I predict you're not only going to feel better and be more energetic, but also you'll decrease your body weight by 2, 3 or even more pounds. [If you do that and care to share your results with me, I'd love to learn of them.]

Is it the most delicious dietary plan? Hardly. *Are you eating for taste or for health and longevity?*

If you are practicing an effective spiritual practice as taught in *Stress Reduction Wizardry*, any need for comfort foods will automatically diminish. Since the rest of your life will be giving you more satisfaction, any desire for comfort foods will automatically be undermined.

Also, when you eat, please sit down, eat in silence, and pay attention to your food. Do not, by way of contrast, be paying attention to something on television or online or to conversation. Avoid being lost in useless thoughts. If you don't, you'll be in danger of shoveling in too much food without even enjoying eating it.

Unless required by a physician, Gundry also argues that it's always a good idea to avoid broad-spectrum antibiotics; nonsteroidal, anti-inflammatory drugs such as Advil, Motrin, Aleve, and Celebrex; stomach acid-blockers such as Zantac, Prilosec, Nexium, and Protonix; artificial sweeteners; genetically modified foods; the herbicide Roundup; and blue light, which is the kind of light emitted by electronic devices such as televisions, mobile phones, computers, LED lighting, and fluorescent lights. (I use relatively inexpensive glasses that filter blue light.) It's best to avoid endocrine disruptors as well. Unfortunately, they are found in lots of products including personal care items, cleaners, plastics, pesticides, food packaging like cling wrap and storage containers, and packaged bread (namely, BHT).

Take breaks from eating. Why not give your gut a restorative rest? Avoid intense exercise while fasting. I recommend intermittent starvation. There are different protocols. Mine has two parts. [i] I fast for 2 or 3 days twice a year. Only consume water, supplements, medications (if any), and, if you prefer, non-sugared tea or coffee for 48 or, better, 72 hours. There's evidence that that may help your body to reset itself (by stimulating stem-cell production). [ii] I fast once a week for 16, 18, or 24 hours without food.

This protocol is not as difficult as you may imagine. With respect to the second part, for example, suppose that you eat dinner Sunday evening at about 6:00 p.m. Just skip breakfast on Monday and don't eat again until lunchtime around noon or until dinner. It's a simple way to enjoy a host of physiological benefits.

Brief periods of intermittent starvation may have spiritual benefits as well as physical benefits. They were undoubtedly natural for our ancestors.

EXERCISING WELL

A similar kind of thinking is applicable to *natural exercising.* How did our hunter-gatherer ancestors move?

The answer was that, when they had to move, they probably moved quickly. Yes, some primitive cultures did considerable walking and some even did considerable jogging. However, around the world, that seems not to have been the norm.

When they moved, they often sprinted to catch something to eat or to avoid being eaten. Did they occasionally have to push boulders or carry a weight like a carcass? Surely. Otherwise, some were likely to have been more physically active than we are but others may have been less physically active than some of us are.

The good news is that, however they moved, we now understand how to exercise well to promote health and longevity.

Recall the importance of VO_2max. As we age, the cells in our lungs begin to die faster than we can replace them. This is alarming because, the smaller our lungs, *the greater our risk of death from all causes.* This is why lung function or capacity is the #1 predictor of death. In that sense, **your ability to breathe well is your ability to live well physically.**

You have a choice: do nothing or do something. If you want to do something, ask 'What can I do to increase my lung function?'

Answer: short bursts of cardiovascular (aerobic) exercise followed by resting signals your body to increase lung capacity. In other words, that's how to improve your degree of cardiovascular fitness. Build lung power by deliberately challenging the capacity of your lungs that way. Of course, if you smoke, quit.

The good news is that *exercise intensity is inversely proportional to duration*. The more intensely we exercise, the shorter the time we're able to exercise. Intense exercise must be brief.

Notice that this is how other animals usually move: short bursts of intense energy expenditure.

High intensity exercise requires large amounts of oxygen, which is the basic fuel your cells require to keep you moving. So, if you have been doing long-distance walking, jogging, or running in an attempt to improve or maintain your degree of fitness (and you have a choice), stop. Continuous cardio is useless for improving VO_2 max.

Instead, do intense interval training. Since it's intense, it must be brief. In fact, a good program [such as the ones in P.A.C.E. in the SUGGESTIONS FOR FURTHER READING below] need not take more than **12 minutes or so two or three times weekly.**

However, that's not the only kind of exercise that is beneficial to your health. Like interval training for improved lung power, strength training not only has physical benefits but psychological benefits.

It, too, should be intense. Therefore, it, too, should not take long. I recommend a program in my Weight Lifting [which is also listed in the SUGGESTIONS FOR FURTHER READING below] that requires **less than 10 minutes weekly** of actual strength training.

Therefore, it's possible to get all the physical exercise required for physical flourishing in less than 1 hour weekly. Is it worth it? Well, it will not only improve your odds of good health into old age but also it leaves you with 167 hours each week for everything else. So, it may add years to your life and vitality to your days.

Permit me to provide some specific examples.

strength training

What follows is a sample routine of the right kind. It's actually the exact routine that my strength training partner and I recently used. We change it every few months. First, we warm up our muscles, connective tissues, and joints (and you can do that daily if you want) and then we do a strength training program 1X weekly. It takes us at least as long to do the stretching and warming up as to go through the strength training program. If you are younger and your body is warm, there's no physiological reason to do as much stretching and warming up as we do.

Any good strength training routine must include either (some version of) squats or (some version of) deadlifts.

Unless you are a beginner (and so weak that you are not seriously stressing your body), doing strength training more than once or twice weekly is very likely to be counterproductive. Remember: you do not grow in the gym. What you do in the gym is to stimulate growth, which occurs only with proper and sufficient rest and nutrition. Become expert at avoiding overtraining.

Unless you are really strong or ingesting anabolic steroids (which I do not recommend for strength training and recommend that you never take them without the advice of a moral physician or surgeon because they can damage your health), training less than every 10 or 14 days is likely to be less than maximally productive and perhaps counterproductive.

The point of physical exercise is to enhance your physical well-being over your lifetime. Accordingly, leave your ego at the door when you enter a gym. If you fail to stay humble, you are quite likely to hurt yourself.

Of course, when it comes to strength training, learn what to do before doing anything. There are, for example, certain exercises that you should never do (for example, behind-the-neck presses or pulldowns) and, similarly, certain exercise techniques that you should never use (for example, bouncing at the bottom of squats).

(I sometimes take some strength training supplements before and after strength training to try to maximize its results. Because I'm not confident enough that they do much good, I won't recommend them here.)

STRETCHING & WARMING UP

pec major mobility; pec minor mobility; cat & dog stretch; hamstring stretch: rotator cuff tennis ball release; lying-knees-together-rocking; thoracic air slides; cobra; femoral triangle tennis ball release; hip circles; 3-plane neck movements; small knee circles; shoulder circles; arm circles; fist exercise; The Egyptian; wrist rotations; elbow circles; spine rotation on chair or bench; full-body lying floor stretch; full squats [bodyweight only; supported in squat rack; weight on heels w shins vertical].

10 back raises on back raise machine using only body weight

35 weighted crunches on ab machine

ROUTINE

The number of sets and reps [repetitions] is not as critical as many people think. The idea is to keep the time under tension to be at least 40 seconds and at most 90 seconds. Physical exercise is unlike spiritual exercise (practice, training). Think of it as like medication: too little is insufficient and too much is counterproductive. Less than about 40 seconds is too little stress to simulate a growth response; over 90 seconds is likely to be too much stress and may actually result to your becoming weaker and decreasing the effectiveness of your immune system. Overtraining is real. Train, don't strain.

Proper exercise form is more critical than many people think. Use perfect form on every rep. Do not use momentum when you are moving weights.

Stationary Zercher barbell hold	45-90 seconds
Renegade dumbbell row on floor	1 set of 15-20 reps

Elbow side plank raise on floor	1 set of 15-20 reps on each side
One-arm dumbbell Z press seated on bench with legs straight	1 set of 15-20 reps on each side
Stiff-legged barbell deadlifts [preceded by multiple warm-up sets]	1 set of 15-20 reps
Dips (to the point where the tops of your upper arms at the bottom of the dip are parallel to the floor or slightly lower)	1 set of 10 reps [If you get stronger and want to do weighted dips, hang the weights from around your neck (as opposed to hanging them off your waist, which will pull your spine apart).]
Pulldowns on lat machine	45-90 seconds

VO$_2$ max training

Do the following or a similar program 3X weekly, unless you do a good strength training program in which case you may reduce the frequency to 2X weekly. That's sufficient, and more might be counterproductive. This is intense exercise, which is a privilege, and it's critical to allow your body sufficient time to recover.

Start slowly. The idea is to work with your body, not to try to force results.

It's particularly important to get your personal physician's blessing before starting this or any similar program. That's especially true if you have any important physical risk factors such as being older than 50; you've not had a physical exam in the last year; you are carrying 25 pounds or more bodyweight than you should be; you are hypertensive; you are taking heart medication; you experience chest pain after exercise; you have lung disease such as asthma or emphysema; you have heart abnormalities such as angina, fibrillation, tachycardia, abnormal EKG, or heart murmur; or you've had rheumatic heart disease.

It's intense, so start slowly and ramp things up over time.

You must use a heart rate monitor. You need to know in advance your resting heart rate, your maximum heart rate during exercise, and your recovery time. (For details on how to calculate these, see Dr. Sears's P.A.C.E.) Without knowing these, you cannot safely do programs like the sample below. (Because I don't want you beginning this program without doing more research, I'm not even going to state here how to calculate them.)

I use a stationary bike. Such relatively expensive equipment, although helpful, is not needed. This is a basic stationary bike workout from P.A.C.E, which is the one book I recommend for understanding how to improve your lung power.

ROUTINE

2-minute warm-up

10 minutes of work plus recovery times

set 1	4-minute exertion + recovery
set 2	3-minute exertion + recovery
set 3	2-minute exertion + recovery
set 4	1-minute exertion + recovery

Hold a little back on the initial sets and give the last set everything you've got for that 1 minute. That's the intensity required to increase your VO_2 max, which, again, is the single best predictor of your future healthfulness. Keep an eye on your heart rate monitor as well as the clock as you exercise.

SUGGESTIONS FOR FURTHER READING
Bradford, D. Compulsive Overeating Help
Bradford, D. Weight Lifting
Diamond, J. The Third Chimpanzee

Evans, W., and Rosenberg, I. Biomarkers
Gundry, S. R. The Plant Paradox
Gundry, S. R. The Longevity Paradox
Koch, R. The 80/20 Principle
Lauren, M., with Clark, J. You Are Your Own Gym
McRobert, S. Build Muscle Lose Fat Look Great
Sanfilippo, D. Practical Paleo
Sears, A. P.A.C.E.
Taylor, J. B. My Stroke of Insight
Tsatsouline, P. Super Joints
Wansink, B. Mindless Eating
Weil, A. Healthy Aging
Wiley, T. S., with Formby, B. Lights Out
Also, "AM & PM Yoga for beginners" [Element DVD].

This is a photo of me in my 60's, which was taken by my training partner in my home gym, doing **stiff-legged deadlifts** for reps with 405 pounds.

❖

Introduction to Living Well Financially

Owning property, including money, is not necessary for living well. It's debatable whether or not working to flourish financially is worth it. Feel free to skip this section.

If you are following the recommendations from the previous sections, you are already doing what is required to be set up to do well financially in the right way.

The most critical question to ask yourself is: "Am I seriously practicing (spiritually) every day?" Mastery requires sustained exertion of the right kind. If so, you are reducing your egocentricity, your attachment to your ego/I. The more you do that, the more you'll be able to focus on what is best for others. The more you focus on what is best for others, the more you'll be able to benefit them by understanding and helping them solve their problems. The more you do that in any way that makes money, the more financial success you'll have. *When you give, it's impossible not to receive.*

Like other kinds of success, financial success leaves footprints. Assuming that you don't want to make all the mistakes for yourself, to whom should you listen?

I use three criteria. First, I don't pay attention to financial advice from people who have a net worth of less than a million dollars (USD). Second, I don't pay attention to people who make money in ways that don't genuinely help people. This rules out, for example, arms dealers and drug pushers. Third, I don't pay attention to those advocating activities that would be ill-suited to my strengths and interests.

Because I'm not a millionaire and never will be, although you might find them stimulating, you'd be wise not to pay much attention to my recommendations in this section.

In general, there are two economies, two ways to attempt to take good care of yourself financially and pay your bills: you can either be an employee or have your own business. Each has advantages and disadvantages. You don't have to choose one or the other: you can do both.

You may be wondering about me. As a philosophy professor, I was for 32 years an employee. That at least shows that I am able to hold a job. I enjoyed continuing appointment (tenure), had a regular paycheck, and relished regular time off. I never made a lot of money, but I enjoyed a lot of freedom, both inside the classroom as well as time off. I wasn't able to write nearly 30 books because I had to work in a salt mine 12 hours a day 6 or 7 days a week! Furthermore, I looked at it like this: partly because I think it can help improve their understanding, I enjoy talking philosophy with those who are seriously interested in living better. I actually got paid for a lot of years to do something I enjoy doing anyway.

Most employees aren't that lucky. They don't get paid to teach. They don't receive adequate pay to do something they'd do anyway. If you, too, have been lucky and enjoy your job, there may be no particular reason to change it or look for ways to supplement your income.

I have made some money having my own businesses. However, I've not yet found a really good business for me, one that really helped others and paid me adequately to do it. In recent years, I've tried multiple different ways of making money as an entrepreneur, but I've not yet been successful. Please, though, don't be misled: I'm very grateful for the opportunities I've had in life. That includes the financial opportunities that have opened up in the last quarter century by the development of the world wide web. I've no complaints whatsoever.

Permit me, though, to recommend one idea that you may find very helpful whether you are an employee or a business owner. It's the idea of a **business friendship.** A business friendship is a kind of what Aristotle called a utility friendship [discussed above in the Introduction to Living Well Morally section]. It's a win/win financial exchange of a product or service.

Suppose, for example, that I own an automobile. It requires regular maintenance and I don't do it myself. Instead, I take it to a local mechanic, Mark, who services it for me. In fact, let's suppose that I've been doing that for several decades. (This is a true story.)

It's a win for me. I know from past experience that Mark is a talented mechanic. He keeps my cars running well. He ensures that they are well-serviced. When one has a problem, he's able to diagnose and fix it properly and correctly. I don't have to search around for the best deals either when, say, my car needs new tires. I simply get them from Mark. He even reminds me when it's time for routine maintenance.

It's a win for Mark, too. The more regular customers like me he has, the less his advertising or marketing costs. He relies on word-of-mouth advertising from satisfied customers like me. Furthermore, he never has to try to convince me that I need something for my vehicles. If my tires can go another six months and I ask him about their condition, he'll tell me that honestly because he knows that, in six months or less, I'll come back in and buy them from him. He offers me special deals, too. For example, when I'm looking to purchase a used car, he'll inspect it for me for free or at a discount. Does that cost him money? In the short term, yes, but not in the long term. If I know that I'm getting a good deal, why wouldn't I go back to him? Furthermore, Mark has always enjoyed working on engines and automobiles. It's fun for him – especially diagnosing and fixing problems. Of course, many tasks related to running a business are not fun, but he does enjoy the basic work and thinks he's getting paid to diagnose and solve problems he enjoys solving while keeping his customers as safe as possible when they are driving.

That's a simple example of a business friendship. If you are already doing quality work of a kind you enjoy and might do for others anyway even if you didn't get paid for it, you're in a perfect position to focus on serving others. If you actually succeed in doing that, you won't ever have to worry about not having enough money. As Zig Ziglar and other successful salesmen have learned, if you help enough others solve their problems then you'll discover that they'll solve all your financial problems.

In 1987 the proportion of Americans who reported being happy with their jobs was 61%, but by 2016 that proportion had fallen to 51% [*The Economist*, 19 Jan 19.]. Assuming that trend has continued, *less than half of employed Americans are happy with their jobs*. (Presumably, most who are unintentionally unemployed are even less happy and more financially distressed.) Why?

One reason may be that wages have failed to keep up with inflation over the last several decades. Another reason may be that economic competition is now worldwide; globalization has meant that increased productivity is required for companies to stay in business. For employees, this makes work more stressful and less enjoyable.

Philosophers distinguish two kinds of justice: *retributive*, which has to do with handling law-breakers, and *distributive*, which has to do with answering the fundamental question that every society faces, namely, "With respect to goods, who should get what?" In other words, how should what is valuable be distributed among the people in a society?

Over a century and a half ago, Marx offered a powerful moral critique of what he called "the property-capitalist system." It has four features according to Marx: it is governed by John Locke's principles of distributive justice, there are no monopolies, there is private ownership of the means of production including labor, and humans are motivated by greed and self-interest.

What is the economic (exchange) value of a commodity in such a system?

The chief idea of Marx's labor theory of value is that, in the long run, the average price of a commodity is determined by the average amount of social labor time necessary to produce it.

The chief idea of Marx's theory of surplus value is that, in the long run, the average price of laboring power (wages) will be the amount necessary to keep the worker alive and working, which is called the "subsistence wage." This is an application of the labor theory of value to one commodity, namely, labor.

Marx is essentially making two claims. First, the wages that an employee gets *must* be less in market value than the increase in market value that he or she adds to products or services. In other words, employers *must* underpay workers or else there would be no company profit and a company would have to go out of business. Second, in the long run, wages will fall toward that subsistence wage below which laborers cannot function well as laborers.

These are both very interesting ideas. Philosophers, economists, and political scientists are still discussing and evaluating them. What I'd like to point out initially is that employees typically feel they are underpaid for the value they create. If you are an employee, you probably feel this way. Without mentioning 'Marx' or 'Marxist' (because Americans have been conditioned against anything so labeled), I myself have asked many employees in different situations over the years whether or not they feel that they are justly rewarded for the value they create. I've not yet encountered an employee who didn't feel underpaid. Score one for Marx about "exploitation" [see below].

Marx's labor theory of value and theory of surplus value are central to his moral critique of the property-capitalist system. There are three chief ideas central to that critique, namely, distributive justice, freedom, and "alienation."

Distributive Justice [Exploitation] Even according to Locke's first principle of distributive justice (namely, "to each according to his work," in other words, employees should be paid for all the value they create), the property-capitalist system "exploits" the worker. Again, unless, for example, a factory owner exploited his employees, there would be no profit. The only alternative within the system would be worse for employees than being exploited, namely, they could be rewarded fairly according to Locke's first principle of distributive justice but then the company would have to go out of business and the employees would lose their paychecks. This is why Marx is not blaming individual capitalists such as factory owners. It's the system that is the problem. It forces factory owners, for example, either to exploit their employees or go out of business. In a property-capitalist system, there is a monopoly of ownership of the means of production and labor is oversupplied. In Marx's theory, the way to end exploitation is to install a socialist system in which the state would own the means of production such as land and factories. Then, since no profits would be necessary, the exploitation of employees would be ended by making their rewards proportional to their laboring activity of creating value. In that sense, Marx thinks that a socialist system would be an improvement over a property-capitalist system because it would be fairer.

However, Locke's first principle is unfair even if workers were not exploited. *Since nature makes humans unequal in their productive capacity, why is it fair to reward them according to their output?* What about the crippled, the retarded, the chronically ill, and others who either cannot produce or must produce less? Furthermore, should workers with large families get the same financial reward as workers with small families? Isn't this simply unfair to children from large families who must then get less? These are serious moral questions about any property-capitalist system; in other words, they are questions of political philosophy.

Freedom The actual real-life situation of the medieval serf and the 19th century factory worker are not substantially different. Neither is free. In fact, the worker is less secure because he may be thrown out of work at any time if the employing company goes out of business. By way of contrast, as long as they fulfilled their obligations to the lord of the manor, medieval serfs had lifelong tenure.

Many people fail to see this because, looking at the world through ideological glasses, they confuse consent with freedom. They fail to understand clearly because their thinking is distorted by their conceptual system. A worker who comes to the bargaining table only with his labor to sell either *must* consent to accept the going wage or not get the job and have no income, which could mean starvation. It's true that employees consent, but that's only because they aren't free to do anything else. The bargaining position of management and labor is inherently unequal.

It seems paradoxical, but workers are freer if the state interferes in the bargaining process by, for example, setting a legal limit to the working day, setting safety standards, restricting child labor, setting a minimum wage, and so on. This, of course, has, in fact, happened in many ways in economically advanced countries since Marx's day. There's no question, for example, that labor unions have often improved the relative financial conditions of employees (and Marx failed to predict their existence). Government programs instituted since Marx's time such as, in the U.S., social security, medicare, and the affordable [health] care act have eased the financial plight of millions.

Again, notice that, according to Marx, it's not individual capitalists who are to blame for the exploitation and lack of freedom of employees. Individual capitalists are no freer than their employees! The blame lands on the whole property-capitalist system itself.

Marx's fundamental question is simple: **since we humans created the system, why can't we create a better one?** A better one would have no exploitation and greater economic freedom.

Alienation As his monster came to dominate the life of its maker Dr. Frankenstein, so the property-capitalist system, which we humans made, has come to dominate our lives. Marx gives the idea of alienation, which he inherited from Hegel and Feuerbach, a new twist. It is we who have lost our place in a world of our own making. **We are blocked from living in our human-made world as we would naturally live.** It is our "conscious life-activity" that distinguishes us from other animals and we naturally express that in free, creative activity by making beautiful things. *This is Marx's most fundamental critique.* He seems to have had an essentially artistic view of human nature. (Note that this is an example of an important point I made above, namely, that a thinker's understanding of human nature has important consequences with respect to that thinker's ethics and political philosophy.) Isn't it bizarre when you stop to think about it that most people spend most of their best waking hours most days of the week having to do work that they'd really prefer not to have to do?

Interpreted in a certain way, there's truth in his conception. In my view, again, all genuine creativity comes from Being [see the "Introduction to Living Well Spiritually" section above]. The good news is that we all share Being as our human essence. What's necessary, though, is realizing that, which requires breaking compulsive thought addiction. Anyone who does that will naturally become more creative.

If you are an employee, as is likely, and at least some of Marx's ideas resonate with you, ask *"What can I actually do to improve my financial condition while minimizing any deleterious effects of my new laboring activity?"*

Could you work to undermine the property-capitalist system and replace it with a better one? Yes, you could try. However, you are very unlikely to succeed. Why? The property-capitalist system is the greatest wealth creator there has ever been in the history of the world. Yes, it's based on greed, which distorts our activities by benefitting those who are successful at being the greediest, and ruthless economic competition [warfare], which often has important unethical consequences, but it does work well to create value. Furthermore, the new system may itself have important unanticipated problems.

You do not have the option of ignoring economic challenges. You must, for example, have water, food, clothing, and protection. However, you could minimize those needs by giving up all private property and, say, joining a monastery or going off into the bush and living more like our hunter-gatherer ancestors. As we have seen, private property is not required for living well. Why? Living well is opening to Being and allowing that to pervade one's life in Becoming. Owning property can be a hindrance to doing that.

However, owning property does have its advantages. If, for example, you don't live in a monastery and are able to own, rent, or borrow a car, you may be able to drive to a location to practice with others who use the same spiritual practice. Similarly, owning a home that is warm in the winter and dry when it rains is a genuine blessing. So, what could you do to improve your lot while remaining an employee?

You may be able to get a different job. Sometimes, especially if it pays more and requires less time and energy than your current job, that's a better option even though it doesn't really solve any of the problems about being an employee.

An excellent alternative is to bring Being into your moment-to-moment laboring activity on the job. Everyone is free to do this and the quality of your work will improve. If the quality of your work improves, so may your pay. From a perspective outside your life, nothing may seem to change. However, from your perspective, everything would change. This option is an excellent one.

Another good alternative is to find a way to improve your work to make it more satisfying. Permit me a true story as an example.

A woman in her 30's, who had graduated college cum laude with majors in both English and philosophy, had become a friend. She had taken several courses I taught. Her work was teaching people how to ride horses. She was going through a difficult time in her life and, somehow or other, she came up with the idea that she might be better off as a physical therapist. She discussed that option with me.

I didn't know or claim to know what she should do. I went online to learn a bit about physical therapy as an occupation. Then I simply tried to help her think through the alternatives more clearly. Basically, I asked her two questions. First, was she prepared to invest the time, energy, and money it would take to go back to college to obtain the scientific background that was required to become licensed as a physical therapist? Second, if so, was she prepared to have physicians control in detail what she could or couldn't do on the job? Yes, her work as a physical therapist would directly benefit her clients and she'd be paid well for that work. However, insurance restrictions would severely limit or eliminate any on-the-job creativity. Other people would have detailed control over everything she did.

She decided to keep giving horseback riding lessons. However, what she did was to contact an agency in her state and began to use those lessons to help troubled children and adolescents, who can find it initially easier to relate to horses than to other human beings. Mastering any skill like horseback riding requires disciplined, persistent training of the right kind. Teaching children that lesson is invaluable to the quality of their lives. It doesn't matter if someone never learns to ride a horse, but it does matter a lot if someone misses the requirements for mastery. Her work became more than just doing something she liked and earning a paycheck. There was a state fund that paid for her services to some students. It became a genuine contribution to the lives of some of her students. (Last I heard from her, and it's been quite a few years, she was still doing that.)

You may be able to create your own side business and become a property-owner. If it's successful, you may be able not only to quit your job but also to spend less time and energy doing work that you dislike. Successful entrepreneurs are not wholly free from the constraints of the property-capitalist system, but they are freer than employees. If a successful factory owner wants to go on a three-month cruise around the world, it's a possibility. It's not for an employee. This is why many argue that profits are better than wages. Starting a successful business is difficult, but it's certainly an option. [Remember video 3 from *Stress Reduction Wizardry*.]

In case you may find my own experience helpful, I'll share it here.

I myself tried to supplement my income as an employee. I tried a number of offline options such as multi-level marketing that didn't work well for me. However, I did hit one that worked, namely, real estate investing. I was a landlord for 30 years, which, in effect, meant that I gave people a good place to live while their rents built up my equity in the apartment buildings. If you educate yourself well before beginning (as I had to do because I couldn't afford any real estate mistakes, which can cost tens of thousands of dollars each), being a good landlord and providing good value to tenants is neither difficult nor time consuming. I was surprised to learn that doing win/win real estate deals can be fun.

I also once tried my hand at flipping houses. I took courses and read books about how to do it. Then I borrowed some money from my retirement fund, purchased a house owned by the FDA's rural development program for so little that it astonished my attorney, hired contractors to make some improvements on the house, bought materials so that my neighbor, who was a professional handyman, and his wife could fix it up, and sold it for a $17,000 profit within six months. I sold it for $34,000 more than the taxes and expenses (including replenishing my retirement fund) on the deal and split that with my handyman. However, because it required constantly being on call, in other words, permitting interruptions, it was not a business well-suited to me.

Ask, 'Could I do something similar?' If you have the ability to pay cash for a fixer-upper and are willing to educate yourself on how to do it well, there's no reason why not.

Ask, 'Could I do something else to supplement my income while genuinely benefitting others?' Why not? What skills do you have that others would pay you either to teach them or to use on their behalf? If you commit to becoming an entrepreneur, it's important to avoid three mistakes.

First, don't underestimate your own abilities. Let's suppose, to pick up on that horseback lesson story, that you understand how to ride horses well. You may not be that talented a rider, but you have enjoyed it for years. Do you realize that, when it comes to teaching beginners how to ride, you have an advantage over more talented riders? It's hard for talented riders to teach beginners because beginners often struggle with things that those who are more talented never struggled with.

Incidentally, it works that way in many fields. How many great professional hockey players have become great hockey coaches? Great coaches in any sport are only very infrequently former great players. In other words, you don't have to be great in a field to be able to teach it well. You just have to be more successful at understanding what to do than your students.

Seriously underestimating your own strengths could hamstring your new business from the start.

Second, understand that the process is: *Learn. Do. Teach.* Let's suppose something unlikely, namely, that you've not yet learned anything that people would pay you to teach them. What could you do?

Have you left the training from *Stress Reduction Wizardry* all in your thoughts or have you begun to practice? If you leave it all in your thoughts, you'll have wasted your time and money. If you have begun practicing, good for you!

Suppose that you began practicing Aliveness Awareness two weeks ago and you are up to doing it for 15 minutes daily. Good, now double that. Soon, double your practicing time again so that you are doing 30 minutes early in the morning and 30 minutes again in the late afternoon or evening. Get so that you really begin to feel the Aliveness intensely each session.

Guess what? You are now qualified to teach others. Why not? It's a simple practice that just takes disciplined effort to master. Everyone can do it. There are no credentials required for being paid as a spiritual teacher.

How could you monetize that?

Why not offer your friends a free meditation lesson? You might run an inexpensive ad in the local PennySaver. You might put an ad in Craigslist or use a video ad in YouTube for your local area. The key is to make it a free lesson.

Get some people to attend. Help them master it. When they begin enjoying success, ask them to tell their friends and give you a recommendation.

Then test the market. Put the word out that you'll give 6 people an hour's lesson for $5 each. If you get them to come, you'll make $30 in an hour, which is more than you paid for either *Stress Reduction Wizardry* or this essay.

If you want to scale up your business, check with your insurance company, your attorney, and your accountant to ensure that you are doing everything you need to do.

Guess what? You just might be a natural teacher. You might really enjoy helping people. If so, that could be a good way to supplement your wages.

You did it the right way, too. You began by learning what to do. You practiced doing it daily. Once you were succeeding, you helped others to succeed. The process is the same in other areas.

Third, what's the most important element in beginning a new business? There's only one right answer: demand. **No demand, no business**.

The great advantage you have if you set up a business teaching Aliveness Awareness is that 99% of people are too stressed. After all, learning how to reduce your own stress in an easy, enjoyable way was what initially attracted you to *Stress Reduction*

Wizardry, wasn't it? Test your local market to see whether 'easy stress reduction' or 'easy meditation' or some similar search phrase [keyword] attracts more prospects.

I'm embarrassed to admit that I failed multiple times to learn the critical lesson of starting with demand. If you fail to start with demand, you'll need to create demand and that's extremely difficult.

For example, consider my website consultingphilosopher. com. It's questionable about how wise I am, but my doctorate in philosophy is supposed to certify that I'm an excellent thinker. Furthermore, I have had experience counseling undergraduates for 32 years (and not infrequently about the quality of their lives and not just about philosophy courses or academic core requirements). Guess what? There is no demand in the United States for consulting philosophers. Perhaps, there should be, but there isn't.

For example, local business owners are busy running their businesses. Furthermore, they now have to compete against, not only the big box stores such as Walmart and department stores such as Macy's, but also against online giants like Amazon. I taught myself how to do digital marketing [cf. ironoxworks.com]. I know that local business owners need help and they know they need help, too. So, now I also have websites [for example, digitalmarketingironox.com and ironoxvideo.com] that are designed to make it easier for local business owners to contact me for my help. Still, it's a struggle. Why? Until they know me, they don't trust me. I know that I can help them make more money from their marketing than my services cost them, but they don't know that and are skeptical because they've been burned before by online marketers. So, it's still a struggle to help local businesses.

The point, though, is that if you start with demand and start small, you may just be successful. Always be testing. *Take small steps and learn from every misstep.* Always be open to going with what is working better and dropping everything else. Let your methodology be the 80/20 rule.

You also now have an advantage over most others in your field. Why? If, as I hope, you have been doing some effective moment-to-moment practice such as Aliveness Awareness daily, you've been diminishing your egocentricity. If you are in business, the more you do that, the more success you'll be able to have. Why?

When doing business deals, you'll be much more effective if you have the empathy to understand the problems your negotiating partner is trying to solve and are able to figure out a creative way to contribute to their solution that may benefit you in the long run as well. That human being on the other side of the negotiating table is not an enemy. He or she is a potential business friend. You share the same essence. Ask questions including, 'How can I help?' Listen patiently and uninterruptedly for the answers. Get him or her talking about life in business. Once you really understand it, let your creativity flow and see if you cannot come up with a win/win solution.

SUGGESTIONS FOR FURTHER READING

Abraham, J. <u>Getting Everything You Can Out of All You've Got</u>
Anderson, C. <u>The Long Tail</u>
Antion, T. <u>Electronic Marketing for Small Business</u>
Carnegie, D. <u>How to Win Friends & Influence People</u>
Cathcart. J. <u>Relationship Selling</u>
Cialdini, R. <u>Influence</u>
Gerber, M. <u>The E-Myth Revisited</u>
Getty, J.P. <u>How To Be Rich</u>
Johnson, S. <u>Who Moved My Cheese?</u>
Kennedy, D. <u>No B.S. Marketing to the Affluent</u>

Kimsey-House, H.; Kimsey-House, K.; Sandahl, P.; and Whitworth, L. Co-Active Coaching.
Kiyosaki, R., with Lechter, S. The Cashflow Quadrant
Kiyosaki, R., with Lechter, S. Rich Dad Poor Dad
Loehr, J., and Schwartz, T. The Power of Full Engagement
Leonard, T. J. The Portable Coach
Maltz, M. Psycho-Cybernetics
Pagan, E. Opportunity
Pritchett, P. Hard Optimism
Rackham, N. Spin Selling
Ries, A., & Trout, J. The 22 Immutable Laws of Marketing
Schwartz, D. J. The Magic of Thinking Big
Williams, R. Secret Formulas of the Wizard of Ads
Ziglar, Z. Zig Ziglar's Secrets of Closing the Sale

ACKNOWLEDGEMENTS

I thank Amber Braun and Dave Pascale for their helpful comments on earlier drafts of this book.

Afterword

We really are all in this together. The key to living better together is opening to Being. Like it or not, you are constantly teaching others. There's no reason not to be the best teacher you are able to be. Open to Being, and teach well.

We need you at your best. Why? Humankind confronts three major challenges and we need to pull together to solve them.

First, there's the threat of nuclear war – as well as the threats of traditional, guerilla, chemical, cyber, and biological warfare – not to mention terrorism. Despite attachment to different views, everyone at least recognizes this problem.

Second, there are the multiple serious threats caused by global warming and environmental degradation. Looming catastrophes such as the warming and acidification of the oceans seem destined to overwhelm humanity in this century partly because, half a century after this problem became obvious to anyone intellectually alive, many seem determined either not to recognize it or not to do anything significant about it.

Third, there are the coming social and economic disruptions caused by technological advances such as machine learning [artificial intelligence], biotechnology, and quantum computing.

It's not just other humans who need you to work on these major and multiple minor problems, other animals also need you. Plants need you. The earth needs you. The universe needs you.

Our essence is divine Being. This means that you and I are not two. **We are God in disguise.** We are here to unleash our creativity by realizing our essential nature.

Dennis E. Bradford

Permit me, friend, to give Walt Whitman the last words, which I selected from his *Song of Myself*:

"There was never any more inception than there is now,
Nor any more youth or age than there is now,
And will never be any more perfection than there is now,
Nor any more heaven or hell than there is now. . .

In all people I see myself . . .

I exist as I am, that is enough,
If no other in the world be aware I sit content,
And if each and all be aware I sit content."

www.ingramcontent.com/pod-product-compliance
Lightning Source LLC
Chambersburg PA
CBHW060115050426
42448CB00010B/1872